Praise for *Citizens of the Empire*

"Robert Jensen supplies a much needed citizens' manual, that explains well the evasion of moral principles that underlie appeals to patriotism, and the differences between nominal and real free speech and a vibrant versus an empty and managed democracy. His justified concerns over his country's and the world's future is meshed with discussion of the basis of hope and the possibilities of constructive action." —Edward S. Herman, author of *The Real Terror Network* and *The Myth of the Liberal Media*

"That the U.S. today is engaged in a project of empire-building is now beyond debate. But few have clarified the consequences and the choice facing those of us who are citizens of that empire: to challenge it peacefully, from within, or to watch aghast as others attack it, violently, from without. Among those who would meet that challenge for justice, there is anger and there is hope. Bob Jensen has managed the unusual accomplishment of describing and invoking both." — Phyllis Bennis, author of *Before and After: U.S. Foreign Policy and the September 11th Crisis* and *Calling the Shots: How Washington Dominates Today's UN*

"Robert Jensen has done it. At a time when world events and domestic politics could understandably lead to fatalism and despair, he has reminded us all what it means to be a human being: to struggle for justice in an unjust society. With a clarity unmatched by most writers today, and with a hopeful tone utterly devoid of the cynicism that often derails progressive voices, Jensen challenges us to face the empire and resist, and reminds us that even when our efforts fail, there is redemption in the struggle itself." — Tim Wise, anti-racism activist, author, Contributing Editor, *LIP Magazine*

"If, as is axiomatic in therapeutic circles, a person suffering psychological disorder cannot begin to recover until s/he acknowledges the fact of his/her illness, the same principle must apply at the level of mass psychology to the populations of entire countries. Robert Jensen not only argues compellingly that this is so in the contemporary United States, he offers the range of proof necessary to convince all but the most delusional among us that his analysis is accurate. Thus does he provide a veritable cognitive tool kit with which to undertake transformation of the lethal pathology afflicting the U.S. body politic into a condition of mental health. *Citizens of the Empire* is vital reading for anyone and everyone who would seek to forge a viable alternative politics in modern America." —Ward Churchill, author of *A Little Matter of Genocide* and *Perversions of Justice*

"Robert Jensen does more than challenge us to think and feel— he also encourages us to transform our lives. While *Citizens of the Empire* provides cogent information and analysis, the book also offers real clarity about the emotional imperatives of coming to terms with grim aspects of the status quo. At the same time that he demolishes media myths about the 'war on terrorism,' Jensen takes apart key mechanisms of propaganda, militarism and convenient illusions. Midway through the first decade of the 21st century, this book will jolt readers into a truer reckoning with their own beliefs and capabilities. Jensen makes a powerful case that we can stop being passive spectators and start being active co-creators of history. *Citizens of the Empire* is a book of realism and hope—a strong antidote to the poisons of conformity and despair." —Norman Solomon, Co-author of *Target Iraq: What the News Media Didn't Tell You*, Executive Director of the Institute for Public Accuracy

CITIZENS OF THE EMPIRE

CITIZENS OF THE EMPIRE

THE STRUGGLE TO CLAIM OUR HUMANITY

BY ROBERT JENSEN

CITY LIGHTS BOOKS
SAN FRANCISCO

Cover design by Yolanda Montijo
Typography by Harvest Graphics
Book design by Elaine Katzenberger

Library of Congress Cataloging-in-Publication Data

Jensen, Robert, 1958-
  Citizens of the empire : the struggle to claim our humanity / by
Robert Jensen.
      p.   cm.
  Includes bibliographical references.
  ISBN 0-87286-432-4
  1. United States—Politics and government—2001-   2. United
States—Foreign relations—2001-   3. September 11 Terrorist Attacks,
2001—Influence.   4. Imperialism.   5. National characteristics,
American.   6. Political culture—United States.   7. Political
participation—United States.   8. Democracy—United States.
9. Progressivism (United States politics)   10. Rhetoric—Political
aspects—United States.   I. Title.
  E902.J45 2004
  973.931—dc22

                                                    2003024354

Visit our website: www.citylights.com

City Lights books are edited by Lawrence Ferlinghetti and Nancy J.
Peters and published at the City Lights Bookstore, 261 Columbus
Avenue, San Francisco, CA 94133.

I know the whole truth there is horrible

It's better if you take a little at a time

Too much and you are not portable

Not enough and you'll be making happy rhymes.

—from "The Gypsy Life," by John Gorka

Dedicated to the ideals

and members

of the Nowar Collective

ACKNOWLEDGMENTS

T HIS BOOK REFLECTS the immeasurable contributions to my political and intellectual life made by Jim Koplin, Rahul Mahajan, and Zeynep Tufekci. My sense of the world and of myself has been dramatically expanded from my work and friendship with them. In different arenas at different times, each has helped me understand what it means to struggle to be a principled person living in the center of the empire. In their own way, each has been my strongest ally, most dependable supporter, and harshest critic.

Special thanks to:

Chuck Spencer, whose continued support, astute editing, and sense of humor have, once again, been especially important;

Sam Husseini, whose questions and answers consistently force me down unexpected but productive paths of political inquiry; and

Pat Youngblood, whose intelligence, hard work, and good nature have made organizing so enjoyable.

Thanks also to those who read drafts of this and other manuscripts, and provided critique, insight, and support along the way: Michael Albert, Phyllis Bennis, Craig Brown, Marcel Coderch, Gail Dines, Beau Friedlander, Hadi Jawad, Romi Mahajan, Adele Oliveri, Justin Podur, Dick J. Reavis, Greg Ruggiero, P. Sainath, Jeff St. Clair, Val Stevenson, Rashmi Varma, and Kamala Visweswaran.

Since 9/11 I have spoken to a variety of campus and community groups around the United States. People always graciously thank me for my efforts, but I benefit far more from these interactions than they do. I am grateful for the chance to see the many ways in which people are struggling to hold onto ideals and are organizing to try to bring those ideals into being in the world. My thanks to all those who have been so hospitable to me and so tireless in their work for a better world.

A version of Chapter 4 appeared as "American political paradoxes: More freedom, less democracy," *Global Dialogue*, 4:2 (Spring 2002), pp. 47-58.

A version of Chapter 5 appeared as "September 11 and the Failures of American Intellectuals" in *Communication and Critical/Cultural Studies*, 1:1 (2004).

CONTENTS

PREFACE

THE WORLDWIDE ANTIWAR actions on February 15, 2003, were the single largest public political demonstration in history. Millions of people all over the globe poured into the streets to try to derail the Bush administration's mad rush to war.

That day's events were the product of months of intense organizing, in which longtime peace-and-justice activists were joined by people new to politics. Vibrant discussions were breaking out everywhere, online and in person. People were taking seriously the duties of citizenship and trying to participate in the formation of public policy. It was a time in which it was possible to have high hopes for a revitalized political culture and the future of democracy.

What was President George W. Bush's response? When asked a few days later about the size of the protests, he said: "First of all, you know, size of protest, it's like deciding, well, I'm going to decide policy based upon a focus group. The role of a leader is to decide policy based upon the security—in this case, the security of the people."[1]

---

[1] George W. Bush, White House news conference, February 18, 2003. Text available at http://www.whitehouse.gov/news/releases/2003/02/20030218-1.html

A focus group? Perhaps the leader of the free world was not aware that a focus group is a small number of people who are brought together (and typically paid) to evaluate a concept or a product. Focus groups are primarily a tool of businesses, which use them to figure out how to sell things more effectively. Politicians also occasionally use them, for the same purpose. That's a bit different from a coordinated gathering of millions of people who took to the streets because they felt passionately about an issue of life and death. As is so often the case, Bush's comment demonstrated his ignorance and condescension, the narrowness of his intellect, and his lack of respect for the people he allegedly serves.

Such is the state of democracy in the United States. The public's servants serve other masters, namely those who control the society's resources and wield real power. Public opinion did not stop the war because our leaders don't treat public opinion as something to listen to but instead something that must be manipulated to allow them to achieve their goals. The groups that made up the antiwar movement had channeled the people's voices, but we had not made pursuing the war politically costly enough to elites to stop it. Because of this, many people who had taken to the streets fell into a state of political depression once that war began. Many felt that February 15 proved that nothing could be done to affect policy, that raw power had won. The system is too clever, too strong, too entrenched, many thought, and there's no hope.

This book is an attempt to respond to those feelings with a realistic assessment of where we are, how we got here, and what we must do to move forward with progressive political work in the United States. My goal is to speak honestly and bluntly about what it has felt like to live in the United States since 9/11 and through the Iraq War, but not get lost in those feelings. The task is to harness those emotions to help overcome the sense of helplessness so many feel and build movements that can translate people's opposition into political power.

Part I of the book looks at three key political slogans, offering a critique of the dominant culture's political mythology and suggesting new ways for progressive people to respond. Part II examines twentieth-century U.S. political history and the contemporary university in an effort to understand how we came to this place and how key institutions have failed us. Part III takes up difficult issues about ourselves and how we live, which we must face if we are to make progress. The book concludes with thoughts on the task we face as citizens of the empire.

There is no reason to be naive about the power of the forces that want to maintain and extend the empire, or about the serious obstacles that progressive people face in struggling to dismantle that empire. It is easy to give in to the temptation to see that struggle as futile, but there also is no reason to be politically paralyzed by the task. The story of human history is full of failure, but also of successes beyond what people ever imagined. We cannot know exactly what will happen if we act. But we know what will happen if we don't. These words of Martin Luther King Jr. about the Vietnam War should haunt us today every bit as much as they did when he spoke them in 1967: "If we do not act, we shall surely be dragged down the long, dark, and shameful corridors of time reserved for those who possess power without compassion, might without morality, and strength without sight."[2]

[2] Martin Luther King Jr., "A Time to Break Silence" in *A Testament of Hope: The Essential Writings and Speeches of Martin Luther King, Jr.*, James M. Washington, ed. (New York: HarperCollins, 1991), p. 243. This speech is also often titled "Beyond Vietnam," and is available online at http://www.thekingcenter.org/prog/non/Beyond%20Vietnam.pdf

INTRODUCTION
9/11: A Moment Lost
Political Emotions: Fear and Anger

W E ALL HAVE stories about where we were and what we felt the moment we first heard about or saw the planes crashing into the World Trade Center. I have one, too. But for me, that wasn't the most important moment of 9/11/01.

My dominant memory of that day is not of the first hours, the moments of shock and horror. I assume that all decent people had similar emotional reactions, rooted in our common humanity. Instead, what I remember most clearly about 9/11 is a moment nearly four hours after the first plane hit the tower.

By that time I was out of class and back in my office, where I was watching the television networks' coverage of events. To give some structure to the chaos of the day, I sat at my computer, watching and typing notes. At 11:43 A.M. central time I was watching ABC's Peter Jennings. He was talking about the response the United States would have to make. To be effective, he said, "The response is going to have to be massive."

By that time, the anchors and reporters on all three broadcast networks I was watching had been talking as if that were obvious. The parade of "experts" who were brought on the air almost immediately to offer instant analysis said the same thing. But there was something that struck me at 11:43 A.M., something in hearing Jennings—usually the least bombastic of the big-three network anchors—acknowledge that, of course there would be a military response, and of course it would be massive.

September 11, 2001, at 11:43 A.M. was the moment in which I knew where we were headed, and I knew it was a mistake. I knew many more people would die, and I knew nothing in the short run was going to stop it.

More than two years later, I remember that moment more clearly than any other from that day. It was the moment in which I realized that the nation had a choice, that the leaders were going to choose the wrong path, that most of the country would go along, and that there would be hell to pay for that choice—by others and, eventually, by us.

Shortly after that I returned to the television. I got on the phone to my closest political friends and colleagues to check in and share first reactions and analyses. They agreed that it appeared the Bush administration would likely use the attacks as a pretext for war, some kind of war somewhere, probably war for a long time. The rest of the day was a blur, as I stayed in my office to monitor the news. That chaotic afternoon gave way to another moment that I recall clearly. Late in the afternoon I realized I would have to write something that night. My friends were gathering to watch the news and talk, but I decided to stay in my office and write.

I wrote out of anger and fear and sadness. I wrote hoping to make some sense out of the day's events. I wrote harshly, because it seemed important to tell the truth that day, even if the truth was harsh. I wrote about U.S. crimes in the past and about my fears of the crimes to come. Everything I wrote in that first essay was the truth as I saw it that day. Two years later, I still believe it to be the truth. (See Appendix for text of this essay.)

Many people since then have said that although they agreed with much of what I wrote that day, they thought it was inappropriate to have published something so harsh so soon. "I like your analysis but not your timing," people told me. But the timing was not my choice. It was dictated by George W. Bush and Donald Rumsfeld, by Peter Jennings and the parade of experts. By the end of that day, the politicians and pundits had made it clear there would be a war. That was their choice, but it was not the only choice.

The United States had been the target of an atrocity, a crime that would make it easy to lash out with massive violence. It would not be hard to manipulate people's anger and fear to justify a war. The policy planners saw that, and they quickly took off the shelf plans they had for expanding U.S. power in the strategically crucial regions of Central Asia and the Middle East. The public would buy war, and the elites could use it to extend and deepen their power. Wars can bolster politicians' standing— especially a president who brought lots of privilege but limited intellect to the job, and was floundering early in his first term. Belligerent rhetoric wrapped in patriotic language would be easy. It was, perhaps, inevitable that the people in power would try to exploit the opportunity. But it was not the only way.

The other path would not have ignored the powerful emotions unleashed on 9/11. People can be afraid, and yet still move deliberately when deciding about policy. People can be angry but choose an appropriate response. People can see that while war is seductive when one feels threatened, it in many cases only increases one's vulnerability. Most important, people are capable of seeing how politicians lie and manipulate. But, unfortunately, the majority of the American people chose war. Some actively sought it out. Many simply accepted it as inevitable. And others turned away to avoid the question. And so it was war. First in Afghanistan, and then in Iraq, and where it stops we do not know.

Those of us who had made a different choice, who wanted a different world, didn't have the luxury of waiting to make our points. When Bush officials made it clear they would give us war, it was clear the resistance would have to begin immediately. The night of 9/11, I could not necessarily have elaborated all these points, but I felt them. I knew that the timing had been determined by others. I would have been happy to have not written that night, to not have been forced to think immediately about the political realities.

Instead, I wrote. At first I wrote just to vent, to help clarify my own thinking. As I did that, it occurred to me that there likely were other people struggling with the same questions. I started to write with more purpose, on the assumption that several left/progressive web sites for which I had written in the past would post my essay. I called my friends and asked them to read a draft; I wanted to make sure what I was writing would not seem crazy to others. After discussion and editing, I sent the piece to the web sites and got ready to go home.

Then, just as I was gathering my things to leave my office, I decided to submit it also to the daily newspapers in Texas for which I have written op/eds in the past. I didn't imagine any of the editors would use it, but I figured it couldn't hurt to send it.

I pushed the send button a few more times and left without giving it another thought.

The morning of September 12, 2001, that essay did appear on several web sites. The morning of September 14, it also appeared in the *Houston Chronicle*, a paper with more than a half-million subscribers. Later that morning a right-wing talk show host in Houston read the piece on the air and encouraged listeners to express their discontent to my bosses at the university. Many of them did. In response, the president of the University of Texas issued a statement distancing the university from me, calling me "a fountain of undiluted foolishness on issues of public policy."[3]

That quick decision to send the essay to the Houston paper set in motion a series of events that changed my life in many ways, that put me in situations I had never expected to face. After the president's condemnation, I had to decide whether I would lay low and be quiet or continue to speak and write and organize. But there really was no decision to make, for there was no way I could stay silent.

Thinking back on it all two years later, I could construct a story about how I made the decision to keep writing and speaking out of nobility, out of a sense of political mission. But the fact is there was nothing noble about it. I made that decision because there was no other decision I could make. I went forward and acted from a set of moral and political values, with a framework of analysis that argued for certain kinds of political action to try to enact those values. I tried to be strategic in my

---

[3] Larry Faulkner, "Jensen's words his own," *Houston Chronicle*, September 19, 2001, p. A-39. Text available at http://www.chron.com/cs/CDA/story.hts/editorial/1053207#jensen

political work, often discussing with friends and allies what should be said at what time and place.

The politics informed my choice, but my emotions made the choice inevitable. One emotion in particular: fear. Despite the fact that sadness dominated that day, it was not sadness that dictated my response. Sadness can be overcome in a variety of ways, many of them in private. If all I had been was sad, either for those who died that day or those I knew would die, I could have coped with that outside of politics. But more than sad, I was afraid. Not afraid that terrorists would get me, but afraid of what might come to be in the world. No matter how many friends and loved ones I could gather around me, nothing could protect me from that fear; it would always seep back into my life. The only way to live with that fear was to act politically, which I did. But I wasn't being noble. I was doing it for myself.

Two years ago, I was terrified of what the men with power (and, even with Condoleezza Rice at the table, they are still mostly men) were going to do. Two wars later, I am more terrified than ever.

That's why, for the past two years, I have been trying to make people more, not less, afraid. When I give talks, I tell people there are real reasons to be afraid; I want people who are hiding from the fear to face it, so that they act. I realized that shortly after 9/11, and I articulated it in the first large public talk I gave, in a church in Dallas.[4] Here is what I said:

> My goal here tonight is simple: I am afraid, and I want you all to be afraid, too. The men in the White House and the

---

[4] "No neutral ground: Alternatives to war," October 8, 2001. The talk was never published but is available online at http://uts.cc.utexas.edu/~rjensen/freelance/attack14.htm

Pentagon have unleashed the dogs of war, but I fear they have unleashed something far worse than any war we have ever seen.

I remember the beginning of the Gulf War. I remember the sadness and fear I felt when that war began. I remember how day by day, as the bodies piled up, I would die a little inside. It was a difficult time. In many ways, I have never recovered from that; it was a harsh coming of age for me.

But this feels different. This feels far worse. This doesn't feel like a war. Let us name what has happened: Not just a war, but a new insanity has been unleashed upon the world. An unlimited war that our leaders counsel could go on indefinitely. A war against enemies in the "shadowy networks," which means we will never know when the shadowy enemy is vanquished. This is quite possibly the policymakers' shot at the final, and permanent, militarization of U.S. society. Add to that the possibility of more terrorist attacks from the fringe of the Arab and Muslim population even more convinced of the depravity of Americans, and the possibility of entire countries destabilized. Are you scared? How can you not be?

This insanity was touched off by the fanaticism of men who believe they understand God's will and have the right to kill to bring about that vision. This insanity has now been furthered by the fanaticism of men who believe they have a right to run the planet by force to protect their privilege.

These men have drawn lines and told us we must choose sides. I will choose sides, but not on their terms. I will choose not just to speak for the peace that our leaders have rejected, but also to speak hard truths about the unjust world that our leaders seek to maintain.

Our president is right; there is no neutral ground.

So, let the men who talk with God and the men who play with power draw their lines. And let the rest of us step outside of the lines into a circle. Let us not only join hands in prayer but also lock arms at the barricades of dissent and civil disobedience. Let us build a movement that can steer a nation off the path of war and onto the path toward justice.

Let us take the president's final words from Sunday and make them our own: "We will not waver, we will not tire, we will not falter, and we will not fail" at the task of our lifetimes, the task of creating justice where there is so much oppression, the task of regaining sanity in a world gone mad.

In this book I want to talk honestly about the emotional and political realities of life after 9/11. I want to examine the intellectual and political collapse of the United States, and confront the sense of alienation and isolation that so many feel in the face of the triumphalism common in the country. The goal in all of this is not to add to anyone's sense of despair, but to face honestly the place we find ourselves so that we can see the reasons we should continue to struggle for justice and understand that we can win.

For citizens of the empire, that struggle is the only way to claim our humanity.

I
CUTTING THROUGH THE FOG OF POLITICAL RHETORIC

I N ANY DEBATE, the person who has the power to set the framework and define the terms has an enormous advantage. Part of the struggle for the antiwar movement, and those taking critical positions more generally, is to avoid being trapped in the rhetoric of the dominant culture.

Especially since 9/11, through the wars in Afghanistan and Iraq, there have been three crucial rhetorical frameworks that have been difficult to challenge in public. All of them are related, but each has to be deconstructed separately. First is the assertion that the United States is the greatest nation on earth. Second is the claim that one must support the troops because they defend our freedom. Third is the assumption that patriotism is a positive value. Anyone who challenges any of these in public in the contemporary United States risks being labeled irrelevant, crazy, or both. But all three claims must be challenged if there is to be progressive political change.

In the next three chapters, I will look in detail at each and suggest a critique. These critiques do not dictate a single political strategy for dealing with these rhetorical frameworks in public. With different audiences and in different situations, different strategies will be appropriate. But it is crucial to be clear about why these ideas are dangerous. Embedded in each are moral and political assertions and assumptions that have to be resisted, which should make progressive political people cautious about buying into the frameworks at all. I will suggest that it's important not just to criticize the dominant culture's version of each claim but to step back and critique the framework itself.

THE GREATEST NATION ON EARTH

ONE OF THE requirements for being a mainstream American politician, Republican or Democrat, is the willingness to repeat constantly the assertion that the United States is "the greatest nation on earth," maybe even "the greatest nation in history." At hearings for the House Select Committee on Homeland Security on July 11, 2002, Texas Republican Dick Armey described the United States as "the greatest, most free nation the world has ever known." California Democrat Nancy Pelosi declared that America is "the greatest country that ever existed on the face of the earth." Even other nations that want to play ball with the United States have caught on. When George W. Bush visited our new favored ally in the Persian Gulf, Qatar, the *Al-Watan* newspaper described it as "A visit by the president of the greatest nation."[5]

I want to offer a different assessment: Any claim to being the greatest nation is depraved and dangerous, especially when made in the empire.

---

[5] Matt Lee and Faisal Baatout, "Bush takes defiant bow before US troops in Qatar, praises reformist emir," Agence France Presse, June 5, 2003.

Sign of pathology

Imagine your child, let's call him Joe, made the declaration, "I am the greatest ten-year-old on earth." If you were a loving parent, interested in helping your child develop into a decent person, what would you say? Let's assume you believe Joe to be a perfectly lovely boy, maybe even gifted in many ways. Would you indulge him in that fantasy? Most of us would not.

Instead, you would explain to Joe that however special he is, he is one of millions of ten-year-olds on the planet at that moment, and that—if there were a measure of greatness that could take into account all relevant attributes and abilities—the odds are against Joe coming out on top. But more important than that, you would explain to Joe that people are a wonderfully complex mix of many characteristics that are valued differently by different people, and that it would be impossible to make any sensible assessment of what makes one person the greatest. Even if you reduced it to a single item—let's say the ability to solve mathematical problems—there's no imaginable way to label one person the greatest. That's why people have so much fun arguing about, for example, who is the greatest hitter in baseball history. There's no way to answer the question definitively, and no one really expects to ever win; the fun is in the arguing.

Now, if Joe makes it to adulthood and continues to claim he is the greatest, we would come to one of two conclusions (assuming he's not saying it just to hype the sales of his book or sell tickets to some event): Either he is mentally unstable or he's an asshole. That is, either he believes it because there's something wrong with him cognitively and/or emotionally, or he believes it because he's an unpleasant person. It's painfully obvious that the best evidence that Joe is not the greatest is his claim to be that, for we can observe that throughout history people who have something in them that we might call "greatness" tend not to proclaim their own superiority.

So, we would want to put the brakes on young Joe's claim to greatness as soon as possible because of what tends to happen to people who believe they are the greatest: They lose perspective and tend to discount the feelings and legitimate claims of others. If I am so great, the reasoning goes, certainly my view of the world must be correct, and others who disagree with me— because they lack my greatness—must simply be wrong. And if they are wrong, well, I'm certainly within my rights as the greatest to make sure things turn out the way that I know (by virtue of my greatness) they should. The ability to force others to accept the decisions of those with greatness depends, of course, on power. If Joe takes positions in society that give him power, heaven help those below him.

All these observations are relevant to national assertions of greatness. Such claims ignore the complexity of societies and life within them. Even societies that do great things can have serious problems. We are all aware that a person with admirable qualities in one realm can have quite tragic flaws in another. The same is true of nations. Constant claims to being the greatest reveal a pathology in the national character. Crucially, that pathology is most dangerous in nations with great economic or military power (which tend to be the ones that most consistently make such claims). That is, the nations that claim to be great are usually the ones that can enforce their greatness through coercion and violence.

Nothing in this argument denies the ways that children or nations sometimes do great things. It is rather the claim to uniqueness in one's greatness that is at issue.

What is greatness?

Let's assume, for the sake of discussion, that determining which nation on earth is the greatest would be a meaningful and useful enterprise. On what criteria would we base the evaluation? And how would the United States stack up? In other words, what is greatness?

We might start with history, where we would observe that the histories of nation-states typically are not pretty. At best, it's a mixed bag. The United States broke away from a colonial power ruled by a monarch, espousing the revolutionary political ideal of democratic rights for citizens. Even though the Founding Fathers' definition of "citizen" was narrow enough to exclude the vast majority of the population, that breakthrough was an inspirational moment in human history. That's why, when declaring an independent Vietnam in 1945, Ho Chi Minh borrowed language from the U.S. Declaration of Independence.

But from the beginning the new American experiment was also bathed in blood. The land base of the new nation was secured by a genocide that was almost successful. Depending on the estimate one uses for the pre-contact population of the continent (the number of people here before Columbus)—12 million is a conservative estimate—the extermination rate was from 95 to 99 percent. That is to say, by the end of the Indian wars at the close of the nineteenth century, the European invaders had successfully eliminated almost the entire indigenous population (or the "merciless Indian Savages" as they are labeled in the Declaration of Independence).[6] Let's call that the first American holocaust.

---

6 See Ward Churchill, *A Little Matter of Genocide* (San Francisco: City Lights Books, 1997). Churchill argues persuasively that the fact that a

The second American holocaust was African slavery, a crucial factor in the emergence of the textile industry and the industrial revolution in the United States. Historians still debate the number of Africans who worked as slaves in the New World and the number who died during the process of enslavement in Africa, during the Middle Passage, and in the New World. But it is safe to say that tens of millions of people were rounded up and that as many as half of them died in the process.

Some would say greatness is not perfection but the capacity for critical self-reflection, the ability to correct mistakes, the constant quest for progressive change. If that were the case, then a starting point would be honest acknowledgment of the way in which the land base and wealth of the nation had been acquired, leading to meaningful attempts at reparations for the harm caused along the way. Have the American people taken serious steps in that direction on these two fundamental questions regarding indigenous and African peoples? Is the privilege of running casinos on reservation land a just resolution of the first holocaust? Are the Voting Rights and Civil Rights Acts an adequate solution to the second? Can we see the many gains made on these fronts, yet still come to terms with lingering problems?

And what of the third American holocaust, the building of the American empire in the Third World? What did the nation that finally turned its back on slavery turn to?

---

large number of those indigenous people died of disease doesn't absolve white America. Sometimes those diseases were spread intentionally, and even when that wasn't the case the white invaders did nothing to curtail contact with Indians to limit the destruction. Whether the Indians died in war or from disease, starvation, and exposure, white society remains culpable.

— The Spanish-American War and the conquest of the Philippines, at a cost of at least 200,000 Filipino lives.[7]

— The creation of a U.S.-dominated sphere in Central America backed by regular military incursions to make countries safe for U.S. investment, leading to twentieth-century support for local dictatorships that brutalized their populations, at a total cost of hundreds of thousands of dead and whole countries ruined.[8]

— The economic and diplomatic support of French efforts to recolonize Vietnam after World War II and, after the failure of that effort, the U.S. invasion of South Vietnam and devastation of Laos and Cambodia, at a cost of 4 million Southeast Asians dead and a region destabilized.[9]

We could list every immoral and illegal U.S. intervention into other nations, which often had the goal of destroying democratically elected governments, undermining attempts by people to throw off colonial rule, or ensuring that a government would follow orders from Washington.[10] But the point is easily made: Subjecting claims of American greatness to historical review suggests a more complex story. The United States has

---

7 See Daniel B. Schirmer and Stephen R. Shalom, eds., *The Philippines Reader* (Boston: South End Press, 1987).

8 See Eduardo Galeano, *Open Veins of Latin America*, rev. ed. (New York: Monthly Review Press, 1997).

9 See Marilyn B. Young, *The Vietnam Wars, 1945–1990* (New York: HarperCollins, 1991).

10 For a comprehensive list, see "That 'Most Peace-Loving of Nations': A Record of U.S. Military Actions at Home and Abroad, 1776–2003," in Ward Churchill, *On the Justice of Roosting Chickens: Reflections on the Consequences of U.S. Imperial Arrogance and Criminality* (Oakland: AK Press, 2003), pp. 39–85; and Zoltan Grossman, "From Wounded Knee to Afghanistan," http://www.zmag.org/list2.htm.

made important strides in recent decades to shed a brutal racist history and create a fairer society at home, though still falling short of a truly honest accounting and often leaving the most vulnerable in seemingly perpetual poverty. At the same time, U.S. policy abroad has been relentlessly barbaric.

Such an examination would lead to some simple conclusions: The United States was founded on noble principles that it has advanced and, often at the same time, undermined. As the United States has emerged as a world power with imperial ambitions—and we rest now at a place where commentators from all points on the political spectrum use the term "empire" to describe the United States, often in a celebratory fashion (more on that in the Conclusion)—we have much to answer for. Historically, empires are never benevolent, and nothing in history has changed that should lead to the conclusion that the United States will be the first benevolent empire. Unless, of course, one believes that God has a hand in all this.

What's God got to do with it?

During the 2000 presidential campaign, George W. Bush was trying to recover from his association with the painfully public bigotry of Bob Jones University. On matters of racism, it's impossible—even for politicians—to make claims about America's heroic history. But in remarks at the Simon Wiesenthal Center and the Museum of Tolerance, Bush said, "For all its flaws, I believe our nation is chosen by God and commissioned by history to be the model to the world of justice and inclusion and diversity without division."[11]

---

[11] "What the US media is saying," *Guardian* (UK), March 7, 2000, http://www.guardian.co.uk/US_election_race/Story/0,2763,193304,00.html

This invocation of a direct connection to God and truth—what we might call the "pathology of the anointed"—is a peculiar and particularly dangerous feature of American history and the "greatest nation" claims. The story we tell ourselves goes something like this: Other nations throughout history have acted out of greed and self-interest, seeking territory, wealth, and power. They often did bad things in the world. Then came the United States, touched by God, a shining city on the hill, whose leaders created the first real democracy and went on to be the beacon of freedom for people around the world. Unlike the rest of the world, we act out of a cause nobler than greed; we are both the model of, and the vehicle for, peace, freedom, and democracy in the world.

That is a story that can be believed only in the United States by people sufficiently insulated from the reality of U.S. actions abroad to maintain such illusions. It is tempting to laugh at and dismiss these rhetorical flourishes of pandering politicians, but the commonness of the chosen-by-God assertions—and the lack of outrage or amusement at them—suggests that the claims are taken seriously both by significant segments of the public and the politicians. Just as it has been in the past, the consequences of this pathology of the anointed will be borne not by those chosen by God, but by those against whom God's-chosen decide to take aim.

What stance on these matters would leaders who took seriously their religious tradition take? Scripture, for those who believe it to be an authority, is—as is typical—mixed on these matters. But certainly one plausible reading of that text would lead one not to claims of greatness but of humility. As one of the Old Testament prophets, Micah, put it: "What does the Lord require of you but to do justice, and to love kindness, and to walk humbly with your God?" (Micah 6:8).

In the second presidential debate on October 11, 2000, Bush himself made this point. When asked how he would try to project the United States around the world, Bush used the word "humble" five times:

> It really depends upon how our nation conducts itself in foreign policy. If we're an arrogant nation, they'll resent us. If we're a humble nation but strong, they'll welcome us. And our nation stands alone right now in the world in terms of power, and that's why we've got to be humble and yet project strength in a way that promotes freedom.
>
> We're a freedom-loving nation. And if we're an arrogant nation, they'll view us that way, but if we're a humble nation, they'll respect us.
>
> I think the United States must be humble and must be proud and confident of our values, but humble in how we treat nations that are figuring out how to chart their own course.[12]

Although all available evidence suggests Bush and his advisers (or any other U.S. president, for that matter) were not serious about pursuing a foreign policy based in humility, his comments were sensible. Humility, it is important to remember, does not mean humiliation; it is a sign of strength, not weakness. It means recognizing that the United States is one nation among many; that the only way to security is to work together democratically with other nations; and that multilateral institu-

---

[12] Second presidential debate, Winston-Salem, NC, October 11, 2000. Transcript available online at http://www.c-span.org/campaign2000/transcript/debate_101100.asp

tions must be strengthened and we must be willing to accept the decisions of such bodies, even when they go against us.

In other words, the exact opposite of the path that the Bush administration has pursued.

Blame America first?

When one points out these kinds of facts and analyses, which tend to get in the way of the "greatest nation" claims, a standard retort is, "Why do you blame America first?" Though it is a nonsensical question, the persistence and resonance of it in the culture requires a response.

First, it should not be controversial that when assessing the effects of actions, one is most clearly morally responsible for one's own actions. Depending on the circumstances, I may have obligations to act to curtail someone else's immoral behavior, but without question I have an obligation to curtail my own immoral behavior. In some circumstances, if someone else's immoral behavior is so egregious that the harm it does to others requires immediate intervention and such intervention is feasible in the real world, then there can be cases in which I have cause to temporarily put on hold an assessment of my own behavior to stop the greater evil. But such cases are rare, and the human tendency to rationalize our own bad behavior should give us pause whenever we claim that the greater good requires us to focus on the mistakes other people make before we tackle our own.

So, in place of the common phrase "judge not and ye shall not be judged," perhaps the rule should be "invite judgment of yourself by others, come to judgment about your behavior, commit to not repeating immoral behavior, repair to the degree possible the damage done by previous immoral acts, and keep an eye on others to help them in the same process."

There is no reason that the same logic that applies to us as individuals should not apply to us collectively as citizens of a nation. From such a vantage point, the emptiness of the accusation that one shouldn't "blame America first" becomes clear. America should be blamed first, if and when America is blameworthy. If the United States has engaged in behavior that cannot be morally justified—such as the invasion of another country to overthrow its legally elected democratic government for the self-interested material gain of some segment of U.S. society— whom else should we blame? Because people often use the term "blame" in a way to redirect accountability (when Johnny blames Joey for breaking the toy, we suspect that Johnny actually had something to do with the accident himself), the phrase is designed to divert people from an honest assessment. A better formulation would be, "Why do you hold America accountable first?" In that case, the obvious answer—we should hold America accountable first when America is responsible—is somewhat easier for a reasonable person to see.

That does raise the question, of course, of who is a reasonable person. We might ask that question about, for example, George H. W. Bush, the father. In 1988, after the U.S. Navy warship *Vincennes* shot down an Iranian commercial airliner in a commercial corridor, killing 290 civilians, the then–vice president said, "I will never apologize for the United States of America. I don't care what the facts are."[13]

Whether the firing was an understandable reaction to the misidentification of the Iranian aircraft (as apologists claim), a

---

[13] Michael Kramer, "What does Bush stand for?" *U.S. News and World Report*, August 22, 1988, pp. 12–20.

deliberate act to send Iran a message about U.S. intentions in the region (as some suspect), or the responsibility primarily of a hyperaggressive, trigger-happy commander (as others argue), Bush's declaration is an extraordinarily blunt admission that he does not adhere to even minimal moral standards. The grotesqueness of the episode was only compounded by the fact that Bush later awarded the ship's commander a Legion of Merit award for "exceptionally meritorious conduct in the performance of outstanding service." We could call it the "blame America never" approach.

The facts matter

My position does not lead to a blanket denunciation of the United States, our political institutions, or our culture. I simply put forward the proposition that facts matter. If we are to be moral people, everything about the United States, like everything about any country, needs to be examined and assessed. People often tell me, "You assume that everything about the United States is bad." But, of course, I do not assume that; it would be as absurd as the assumption that everything about the United States is good. After a lecture in which I outlined some of the important advances in the law of free speech in the United States but was also critical of contemporary U.S. foreign policy, someone in the audience asked, "Is there anything about America that you like?" Yes, I said, there is much I like—for example, the advances in the law of free speech that I just spent considerable time describing and celebrating. For some reason, honest assessments of both the successes and failures of the United States are seen as being hypercritical and negative.

The facts do matter, of course. And the "greatest nation on earth" mantra tends to lead us to get the facts wrong. Take the question of foreign aid. One would assume that the greatest nation on earth, which also happens to be the wealthiest nation on the planet with the largest economy, gives generously to nations less fortunate. And, in fact, many Americans do assume that. Unfortunately, it's wrong. Political journalist William Finnegan summarizes the polling data:

> Americans always overestimate the amount of foreign aid we give. In recent national polls, people have guessed, on average, that between 15 and 24 percent of the federal budget goes for foreign aid. In reality, it is less than 1 percent. The U.N. has set a foreign-aid goal for the rich countries of .7 percent of gross national product. A few countries have attained that modest goal, all of them Scandinavian. The U.S. has never come close. Indeed, it comes in dead last, consistently, in the yearly totals of rich-country foreign aid as a per centage of GNP. In 2000, we gave .1 percent. President Bush's dramatic proposal, post-September 11, to increase foreign aid to $15 billion looks rather puny next to the $48 billion increase in this year's $379 billion military budget.[14]

So, on this count, are the Scandinavian nations the greatest on earth? They also seem to have the edge on us in providing health care to their citizens. Here's the assessment of two prominent U.S. medical researchers:

> The absence of universal access in the United States is a global scandal. No other highly industrialized country has so many citizens totally without access to even the most rudimentary health care. Consider these facts: there are almost

---

[14] William Finnegan, "The economics of empire," *Harper's Magazine*, May 1, 2003.

> twice as many people in the U.S. without access to health care than the entire population of Scandinavia where access is a universal right.[15]

One might think that the greatest nation on earth would not leave its most vulnerable citizens without reliable access to health care. There will be, of course, disagreement on how to best achieve that, but it seems not to be a serious goal among the dominant political players in the United States.

So, we score higher on legal guarantees of freedom of speech but lower on guarantees of health care compared with other developed countries. Our history and contemporary foreign policy suggest that self-interest and greed usually trump concern for human rights and democracy. Yet the existence of a democratic process at home—the product of much struggle by the forces interested in progressive change—should leave us with hope that we can change the course of that policy through long-term, dedicated efforts. But to do that, honest reflection on the record is required. And it matters. It really matters. It is one thing for small and powerless nations to have delusions of grandeur; they can't do much damage outside their own borders. It is quite another thing for the nation with the most destructive military capacity in the history of the world—and a demonstrated willingness to use it to achieve self-interested goals—to play the "greatest nation on earth" game. To the degree that the game diminishes people's ability to assess facts, reach honest conclusions, and take moral action based on those conclusions, it increases the risk of people everywhere. It makes

---

[15] Gordon Schiff and Quentin Young, "You can't leap a chasm in two jumps," *Health Letter*, December 1, 2001.

it easier for leaders to justify wars of conquest and mask the reasons for those wars. It's easy for a vice president to say, as Dick Cheney did in a speech in 2002:

> America is again called by history to use our overwhelming power in defense of our freedom. We've accepted that duty, certain of the justice of our cause and confident of the victory to come. For my part, I'm grateful for the opportunity to work with the president who is making us all proud upholding the cause of freedom and serving the greatest nation on Earth.[16]

---

[16] Dick Cheney, National Republican Congressional Committee salute to retiring members of Congress, October 2, 2002.

SUPPORT THE TROOPS

THE DEMAND DURING the Iraq War that—whether for or against the war—one must support the troops was the most effective type of rhetorical strategy: Simply by accepting that framing of the question, opponents of the war were guaranteed to lose the debate, and the chance for meaningful political dialogue would evaporate. So, when asked, I tried to refuse to answer the question of whether or not I supported the troops. Instead, I said that I don't support the "support the troops" framework. That doesn't mean I don't like the troops (of the troops I have known, I have liked some and disliked others, as is the case with every group of people I've ever run into). It doesn't mean I wish to see any of them harmed physically. But I don't support talking about whether I support them.

Here's a concrete example: The semester before the Iraq War I had in one of my classes a student, let's call her Jane, who often stopped by my office to talk about material from the course, especially concerning media and politics. We shared some views but differed on a number of issues, and I enjoyed the exchanges. Jane also was an officer in the Army Reserve, and she expected to be called up for the war. Late in the semester she stopped by to tell me she would not be back the next term.

Though she was conflicted about the war, Jane had legal obligations to the Reserve, and she intended to fulfill them. I understood the position she was in, and it was clear she did not intend to make a political statement by refusing active duty, nor did she intend to ask for conscientious objector status or alternative duty. She also knew that I opposed the war on moral, legal, and political grounds. So, there we sat. At that moment, if someone had told me that I must support the troops—or in this case, support the one very specific troop who was in front of me—what would that mean? Should I have told her that I supported her decision to go fight in a war I believed to be immoral, illegal, and unwise? Should I have supported Jane by denying my own conscience? What good would that do her or me, the country or the world? Certainly I could, and did, tell her that I understood the difficult position she was in. But if the critique of the coming war that I had been voicing for several months had been sincere, what would it mean for me to say to her, "I support your decision"? It would be a transparent lie. I couldn't support her decision, no matter how much I understood the reasons she was making her choice.

The implicit demand in the "support the troops" rhetoric was—and likely will be in future wars—that even if I am against the war, once troops are in the field I should shift my focus from opposition to the war to support for my fellow Americans who are doing the fighting. But to support the troops is, for all practical purposes, to support the war. Asking people who oppose a war to support the troops in that war is simply a way of asking people to drop their opposition. If I had believed this war would be wrong before it began, and if none of the conditions on which I based that assessment had changed, why should I change my view simply because the war had started?

In a democratic society, the question should not be whether one supports the troops. The relevant question is whether one supports the policy. The demand that war opponents must "support the troops" is nothing more than a way of demanding that we drop our opposition to the policy.

Attempts at rhetorical resistance

Many war opponents responded to the challenge by arguing that they were supporting the troops, first by trying to derail a war so that troops would not have to fight, and later by bringing the war to a close as quickly as possible. The sentiment behind that response is understandable, but I believe it is the wrong approach, in part because it implicitly accepts the legitimacy of the "support the troops" framework. But more important, it's a disingenuous answer because it doesn't take seriously the decisions made by the troops themselves.

An analogy: Let's say I have just joined a religious group that is led by a charismatic figure and seems to have all the markings of a cult. I am enthusiastic about this choice, and I am devoting all my available time and energy to the group. I discuss this with friends and tell them I would like their support. Fearing what will happen to me if I give my life over to a cult, they offer a critique of the group, its theology, and its mode of organization. I listen but am not persuaded, and I repeat my request for support. At that point, my friends tell me they support me but they can't support my decision to join this group because they believe it to be a bad decision. In such a circumstance, I would argue to them that support for me as a person is an abstract concept that, while appreciated, doesn't mean much in the immediate situation. What I want, I would repeat, is support in this endeavor I have chosen.

My friends might tell me that their questioning of the wisdom of my choice is a kind of support. I would point out that it is not support but an assertion that their judgment is better than mine and that I should rethink my choice. There's nothing wrong with friends making such assertions; in fact, that is one important role friends play. But, I would conclude, it isn't the same thing as support. It is refusing to support my choice on the basis of an assessment that my friends believe to be superior to my own. Now, if I'm the only person affected by my decision, and I'm a generally competent adult capable of making my own decisions, my friends should accept my choice and drop the issue. From there, we may or may not remain friends, depending on how I behave and how my friends react. But if my allegiance to my new group had detrimental consequences for others—let's say it led me to abandon support for my child, leaving him at risk—then it would be appropriate for those friends, no matter what their desire to support me in some general sense, to take actions to prevent the harm to others in whatever way is appropriate and feasible.

The same points apply to the question of supporting the troops. First, my argument assumes that most people in the U.S. military believe they are serving in a morally sound institution. Of course they have their complaints about that institution, but that typically does not translate into fundamental questioning of the role and mission of the armed forces. The increasing dissension among the troops and their families during the occupation of Iraq, for example, seems to be rooted for most not in a deep critique of U.S. foreign and military policy but in exasperation about a confusing situation and difficult conditions on the ground. No doubt there are members of the military who have come to the conclusion that a specific war—or perhaps even the fundamental nature of the contemporary U.S. armed forces—cannot be justified, but that is a minority, and likely a tiny minority.

So, if I am to be sincere in my position and also respect the troops' capacity to make their own decisions, I can't support them. I can only say that as a fellow citizen, I believe their choice to be wrong, and that while I support them in some general sense—that is, I don't wish to see harm come to them—I do not, and cannot, support them in the choice they have made. I can point out that I realize the decision to pursue war was made by others far above them in the hierarchy. I can express solidarity with those in the military who joined out of economic necessity. But because I believe that the consequences of the war will be harmful to others, I am morally obligated to continue my opposition. I do that fully aware that an ongoing opposition movement in the United States will be taken by many in the military as a betrayal, especially as they risk their lives in combat. I could offer a stirring defense of dissent in democracy, but that is unlikely to be compelling to the troops, given their circumstances. Given that, it is particularly empty to tell troops who believe I am not supporting them that I really am but they just don't understand it.

If we are to use the words "support" and "oppose" with their common meanings, I did not support the troops in the Afghanistan and Iraq Wars. I opposed the troops. And I will continue to do so when I believe they are engaged in immoral, illegal, and unwise conflicts.

Defending your freedom

People who are not convinced by such an argument often respond by making a second claim: I should support the troops because they are defending my freedom, and hence I have an obligation to be loyal to them. Two questions arise from that claim. First, is the conflict in which the troops are fighting actually being fought to defend the freedom of Americans? And, if it were the case that the freedoms of Americans were at risk, is a war the best way to defend them?

In the case of the Afghanistan and Iraq Wars—and every other conflict fought in my lifetime (I was born in 1958)—the freedoms of Americans were not at risk. Put bluntly: American troops have never fought for my freedom (and, since the War of 1812, the only conflict about which one can even attempt a reasonable argument about this is World War II). Many Americans, whether they have served in the military or not, not only disagree with that assessment but have trouble even engaging the question. Several months after 9/11, I participated in a panel discussion on the war in Afghanistan, during which I said that I thought it was time for Americans to come to terms with a harsh reality: In the post–World War II world, a primary function of the U.S. military has been to kill mostly nonwhite people in the Third World to extend and deepen American power. A man in the audience who had served as an army officer took offense and said, with considerable passion, that all those nights he had been on duty in Europe during the cold war he knew he had been defending the American people and American values.

I tried to explain the context of my comment. For most of the post–World War II era, the U.S. use of force against weaker nations was justified as necessary to stop alleged Soviet plans for world conquest. It's true that the Soviet regime was authoritarian, brutal, and interventionist in its own sphere, and it eventually acquired the capacity to destroy us with nuclear weapons (after, of course, we had developed and used such weapons). But the claim that the Soviet Union was a global military threat to our existence was a political weapon to frighten Americans into endorsing wars to suppress independent development in the Third World and accepting a permanent wartime economy.[17] With the Soviet Union gone, American planners needed a new justification to keep the military machine running. International terrorism and threats from drug traffickers were tested as rationales during the 1980s as the Soviet threat receded. In the 1990s, talk of "humanitarian interventions" also became a justification for a bloated military that was far beyond the level needed for defense. On 9/11, the vague terrorism justification became tangible for everyone. So, even if nonmilitary approaches to terrorism are more viable, the rationale for ever-larger defense spending was set. But none of that has anything to do with freedom, ours or theirs.

I wanted to talk more with the man, but he left before the program was over. I would have told him that I was not suggesting that he was inauthentic in his defense of the military or his participation. Instead, I had a different analysis, which led the two of us to different conclusions. In a functioning democracy, such differences over facts, analysis, and future policy choices should be as robust as possible. To accomplish that, difficult discussions are inevitable; such conflicts can't, and shouldn't, be avoided. In other words, I have no doubt that he sincerely believed that as a member of the U.S. military he was defending our freedom, an honorable goal we should respect.

---

[17] See Noam Chomsky, *World Orders, Old and New* (New York: Columbia University Press, 1996), "The Cold War Reconsidered," pp. 26–74.

My argument was that as a member of the military he ended up serving a government with a different objective—to shore up U.S. power and guarantee the profits of an elite, a goal I do not support. There is no disrespect in asking fellow citizens who have joined the military to question, "What am I really fighting for?" and "Who really benefits from the risks I take?"

Responding to the terrorist threat

Certainly Americans and others are at risk because of international terrorism. Here, the second question—is a war the best way to defend the United States—becomes relevant. Shortly after 9/11, Rahul Mahajan and I wrote an essay that advocated a two-track strategy for responding to the attacks. First, a vigorous law-enforcement response, drawing on the resources not only of domestic but international agencies, was needed. Such endeavors are far more effective in fighting terrorism than war. As Mahajan put it in a subsequent analysis:

> It is, however, the Bush foreign policy that has been most detrimental to fighting the threat of al-Qaeda-style terrorism. The war on Afghanistan, judged purely as an anti-terrorist exercise, has been the worst failure of all. First, if you're trying to catch individuals, extradition has a much higher probability of success than war. Dropping 2,000-pound bombs is not the smartest way to go looking for criminals. It will kill a few of them, but not only will many innocent people get killed, the confusion and the hundreds of thousands of new refugees created by the bombing will allow small bands of well-organized people to slip away. And, in fact, the war did not result in the apprehension of Osama bin Laden or any other high-level al-Qaeda leader, although Mohammed Atef, one of the military leaders, was killed. In fact, the most significant members actually apprehended, like Abu Zubaydah

and Khalid Shaikh Mohammed, have been caught by undramatic, routine police operations.[18]

But after 9/11, proposing a police operation alone would not be enough. Five weeks after the attacks, Mahajan and I wrote the following. It seemed sensible then; two years later, with the Iraq war added to the mix, it seems even more sensible.

[T]he United States should do what is most obviously within its power to do to lower the risk of further terrorist attacks: Begin to change U.S. foreign policy in a way that could win over the people of the Islamic world by acknowledging that many of their grievances—such as the sanctions on Iraq [which were eventually lifted after the invasion of Iraq], the presence of U.S. troops in Saudi Arabia, Israel's occupation of and aggression against Palestine—are legitimate and must be addressed.

This shouldn't be confused with "giving in to the terrorists" or "negotiating with bin Laden." It is neither. It is a practical strategy that demonstrates that a powerful nation can choose to correct policies that were rooted in a desire to extend its dominance over a region and its resources, and are now not only unjust but untenable. It is a sign of strength, and it is the right thing to do.

Some have argued against any change in U.S. foreign policy in the near term. International law expert Richard Falk wrote in *The Nation*, "Whatever the global role of the United States—and it is certainly responsible for much global suffering and injustice, giving rise to widespread resentment that at its inner core fuels the terrorist impulse—it cannot be addressed so long as this movement of global terrorism is at

---

18 Rahul Mahajan, *Full Spectrum Dominance: U.S. Power in Iraq and Beyond* (New York: Seven Stories Press, 2003), p. 33.

large and prepared to carry on with its demonic work."

In fact, the opposite is true: Now is precisely the time to address these long-term issues.

Here we can actually take a page from "liberal" counterinsurgency experts who saw that the best way to defeat movements of national liberation was to win the hearts and minds of people rather than try to defeat them militarily. In those situations, as in this one, military force simply drives more people into resistance. Measures designed to ease the pressure toward insurgency, such as land reform then and changing U.S. Middle East policy now, are far more likely to be effective. The alternative in Vietnam was a wholesale attempt to destroy civilian society—"draining the swamp" in Donald Rumsfeld's phrase. The alternative now would be unending global war.

In the past, such strategies were part of a foreign policy "debate" in which the end goal of U.S. economic domination of Third World countries was shared by all parties, and so they were entirely illegitimate. Now, it is different—these terrorists are not the voice of the dispossessed and they are not a national liberation movement. Their vision for their own societies is grotesque.

But they do share something with the wider populace of their countries.

There is tremendous justified anger in the Islamic world at U.S. foreign policy. For the vast majority of the populace, it has not translated to anger at the United States as a nation or at Americans as a people. For groups like al-Qaeda, it has. Their aims and methods are rejected by that majority, but the shared anger at U.S. domination provides these terror networks their only cover. A strategy to successfully "root out" those networks must isolate them from the populace by eliminating what they hold in common. It is necessary to get the cooperation not just of governments of Islamic nations but of their people as well. The only way is to remove their sources of grievance.

These changes in policy must be preliminary to a larger change. The United States must drop its posture of the unilateralist, interventionist superpower. In lieu of its current policy of invoking the rule of law and the international community when convenient and ignoring them when it wishes, it must demonstrate a genuine commitment to being bound by that law and the will of the international community in matters of war and peace.

Many have said of the Afghans, and perhaps by extension of many other deprived peoples, "Feed them and you'll win them over." This attitude dehumanizes those people. Nobody will accept bombs with one hand and food with the other. Nor will anyone feel gratitude over food doled out by an arrogant superpower that insists on a constant double standard in international relations and makes peremptory demands of other nations on a regular basis. To win the support of Afghans and others for the long term, which will be necessary to substantially reduce the danger of terrorism, the United States must treat other peoples with dignity and respect. We must recognize we are simply one nation among many.

This strategy will not win over bin Laden or other committed terrorists to our side; that's not the objective. Instead, we have to win over the people.[19]

---

[19] Rahul Mahajan and Robert Jensen, "Hearts and Minds: Avoiding a New Cold War," October 18, 2001. This essay first appeared on several web sites, including the Common Dreams News Center, http://www.commondreams.org/views01/1018-07.htm. It was reprinted in Anna Kiernan, ed., *Voices for Peace: An Anthology* (London: Scribner, 2001), pp. 171–177.

Empathy, not support

One of the best qualities of human beings is our capacity for empathy, which we should attempt to engage—while understanding that we routinely will fail—in all relationships. What opponents of a war owe the troops is not unquestioning support that undermines our moral and political judgments but a heightened sense of empathy, given the situations those troops will find themselves in. Whatever conclusions we reach about a war, we certainly can understand that those who fight wars face horrific choices about life and death, and often live with routine deprivations that no one wants to face. Empathy does not mean a burying of differences, but an attempt to transcend differences to understand more fully the position members of the military are in.

On this count, it is the contemporary U.S. military—as an institution—that is lacking, not the antiwar movement. Periodic scandals over neglect of the health and welfare of active-duty military personnel and veterans—the most notorious of which are the government's foot-dragging on Agent Orange[20] and Gulf War Syndrome[21]—are commonplace. While the Bush administration was riding high on the wave of pro-military patriotism, it submitted a fiscal 2004 budget that aimed to cut $6.2 billion in veterans' funding over ten years.[22] There are many reasons to believe that the commitment of political

---

[20] See work of Vietnam Veterans of America, http://www.vva.org/benefits/vvgagent.htm

[21] See work of National Gulf War Resource Center, http://www.ngwrc.org/

[22] Kathy McCabe, "Veterans up in arms over proposed cuts," *Boston Globe*, April 24, 2003, p. A-1.

leaders to members of the military does not necessarily correlate with those leaders' willingness to commit those same people to battle.

Beyond those affronts, it's not clear that those commanding the troops are capable of this empathy. At the highest levels, certainly many officers are well aware of the role of the U.S. military in securing and expanding the American empire abroad in the twentieth century, especially the post–World War II era.[23]

No matter how much they have internalized the American mythology and the "defending our freedom" rhetoric, they have enough direct experience with power to know better. What effect does that have on their ability to empathize? Consider this exchange between George Stephanopoulos of ABC News and General Tommy Franks in April 2003 on the Sunday morning talk show *This Week*. The bulk of the interview consisted of Stephanopoulos throwing the general softball questions about the U.S. victory in Iraq. But near the end, Stephanopoulos asked one insightful question:

> Stephanopoulos: You now have a lot of soldiers under your command who have killed for the first time, about to go home, and I want to read you something that one of them told *The Christian Science Monitor* after a battle near Najaf, where wave after wave of Iraqis were killed. This is what he said, "For lack of a better word I feel almost guilty about the massacre. We wasted a lot of people. It makes you wonder

---

[23] For one of the most honest acknowledgments of that by an officer, see "War Is a Racket," Major General Smedley Butler, http://www.ratical. org/ratville/CAH/warisaracket.html. Butler retired from the Marine Corps in 1931.

how many were innocent. It takes away some of the pride. We won, but at what cost?" How do you answer that soldier? [24]

Franks: I don't think, I don't think you give a good discrete answer that says anything more than you've done your duty. You have proven one more time for the world to see that we are a humanitarian people above everything else, not only do we have an incredibly powerful military and, George, we do, but we also have case after case after case of the American soldier who has been in a heck of a firefight take the first prisoner and the first thing he does with the prisoner is hand him a bottle of water, maybe hand him a pair of socks. And so to this, to this specific soldier, what I would say is, you've done your duty and your nation thanks you. [25]

The U.S. attack on Iraq was a contest between the most powerful military in the history of the world that possesses the most sophisticated weapons ever developed, and a Third World nation weakened to the point of collapse by two previous wars and thirteen years of the most brutal economic embargo in modern history. In such a conflict, the dominant military force is going to often find itself in situations where it can literally destroy everything in its path, and sometimes it will. The soldiers who do that killing are far from home, fighting for a cause that is, at best, morally ambiguous. One might think that the top commander of such a military force would have given some thought to that reality and what it would mean for the troops, whose interests he is said to value greatly. In a friendly television interview, with a journalist not interested in asking critical ques-

---

[24] The quote appeared in Ann Scott Tyson, "US troops' anguish: Killing outmatched foes," *Christian Science Monitor*, April 11, 2003, p. 3.

[25] ABC News *This Week*, April 13, 2003.

tions, it is quite extraordinary that the best that general could come up with when faced with that question was, "you've done your duty and your nation thanks you."

It's difficult to imagine that the general's comments would have helped the young soldier cope with his guilt.[26] Maybe there is nothing that anyone could say that would significantly change how that young man felt. I have never killed and never had to deal with the psychological aftermath. But, even without that experience, I am fairly certain that Franks's words fell short of the kind of empathy that might have helped that young man and others like him. I am not arguing that Franks does not care about the men and women under his command; instead, I would suggest that Franks is in a position that makes real empathy difficult if not impossible. Such empathy in that situation requires acknowledging the truth about the war, and if Franks could acknowledge such truth on national television, he would have never gotten to be a general.

Some might consider me the least likely person to be able to communicate with people in the military. To the best of my recollection, I never once in my life considered joining the military. Although not from a wealthy family, I never had to consider the military to finance my college education. Only one contemporary friend or loved one, my younger brother, has served in the military while I knew him. I have opposed every U.S. war since I was old enough to form an opinion, and I'm a leftist. In the

---

[26] The lack of attention to this subject prompted Lieutenant Colonel Dave Grossman, a psychologist and twenty-year Army veteran, to research killing in the military. He argues for a "resensitization of America." See *On Killing: The Psychological Cost of Learning to Kill in War and Society* (Boston: Little Brown, 1995), p. 325.

eyes of most people, I have little or no standing to weigh in on such questions. Yet, I would argue, people like me have more potential for empathy than Franks.

Some soldiers might agree. As U.S. troops in Iraq in the spring and summer of 2003 began to face increasing Iraqi resentment of their occupation of the country, those soldiers came under increasing stress. Some admitted to shooting indiscriminately at civilians and killing wounded prisoners. And some were willing to acknowledge their disgust with their leadership: "We're more angry at the generals who are making these decisions and who never hit the ground, and who don't get shot at or have to look at the bloody bodies and the burnt-out bodies, and the dead babies and all that kinda stuff."[27] As another soldier put it, "If Donald Rumsfeld was here, I'd ask him for his resignation."[28]

If those soldiers were to look to the civilian commander-in-chief, what would they hear? As attacks on U.S. soldiers mounted during the summer of 2003, Bush blustered, "We've got the force necessary to deal with the security situation." He defiantly challenged Iraqi militants striking at U.S. forces: "Bring them on."[29] That might strike soldiers as an easy challenge to offer, sitting in Washington, D.C.

If I had to face these young men, I would begin by acknowledging that if we lived in a decent world, what they had been asked to do and what they did in Iraq would be unthinkable. In

---

[27] Bob Graham, "I just pulled the trigger," *Evening Standard* (UK), June 19, 2003. http://www.eswheels.co.uk/news/articles/5402104

[28] *ABC World News Tonight,* July 15, 2003.

[29] "Bush defiant in face of Iraqi attacks," Agence France Presse, July 3, 2003.

a decent world, the weapons they fired would never have been invented and the military in which they served would not exist. But, instead of a decent world, we live in a world where the demands of power put them in Iraq, with those weapons in their hands, facing those doomed Iraqis. I would have told them that, while I didn't know what they had faced, I knew that others had faced it—and faced the truth—and come through it.[30]

And I would, as respectfully as possible, tell people serving in the military that throughout history there has been not just a patriotic call to war but also a call to resistance, a plea for solidarity among ordinary people who want to build a better world, not serve the empire. It is a reminder, as John McCutcheon put it so eloquently in song, that "the ones who call the shots won't be among the dead and lame / And on each end of the rifle we're the same."[31]

[30] Daniel Hallock, *Hell, Healing and Resistance: Veterans Speak* (Farmington, PA: Plough Publishing, 1998).

[31] John McCutcheon, "Christmas in the Trenches," Appalsongs, ASCAP, 1984. From the album *Water from Another Time,* 1989.

PATRIOTISM

IN ONE OF their "Campaign for Freedom" public-service television ads created after 9/11, the nonprofit Ad Council captured the mood of a sizable segment of the American population in an ad that begins with a shot of a row of average houses. In somber tones, the voice-over says: "On September 11, terrorists tried to change America forever." The shot fades into a new picture of the same street, this time with U.S. flags flying from every home. "Well, they succeeded," the voice concludes, followed by the slogan of the campaign: "Freedom. Appreciate it. Cherish it. Protect it."

For many, that was the patriotic equation: United States = Freedom = Flag. The conventional image was of a sleeping giant wakened, ready to assert itself in the world, its people brimming with a revitalized sense of patriotism. Such declarations came from virtually every politician and pundit.

And also, to the surprise of some, it came from many in the antiwar movement, who declared, "Peace is patriotic." In the struggle to avoid marginalization—in an attempt to find some rhetorical device that could get traction in mainstream America—many who opposed the U.S. attacks on Afghanistan and Iraq did not argue against patriotism, but instead struggled over the way patriotism should be defined. When faced with the claim that patriotism meant supporting the nation as it went to war, antiwar organizers responded that dissent and critique of an immoral, illegal, and counterproductive war also were expressions of patriotism. These activists tried to distinguish between a reflexive nationalism (my country, right or wrong) and a reflective patriotism (my country, as we try to make it better), framing the former as inappropriate for a democracy and the latter as the best expression of democracy.

A similar debate went on within journalism. There were differences of opinion about whether journalists should publicly proclaim their patriotism and about how aggressive the questioning of officials should be in certain situations. CBS News anchor Dan Rather took flak for various hyperpatriotic comments he made after 9/11, most notably his September 17, 2001, remark on the David Letterman show: "George Bush is the president. He makes the decisions, and, you know, it's just one American, wherever he wants me to line up, just tell me where, and he'll make the call."[32] But Rather was no doubt accurate when he told a newspaper convention in March 2002, "[W]e all want to be patriotic."[33]

Bill Kovach, chairman of the Committee of Concerned Journalists, was one of the strongest mainstream spokespersons for a tough, critical journalism after 9/11. He did not trumpet patriotism, but endorsed the concept in his defense of journal-

---

[32] L. Brent Bozell, "Media coverage at its best," *Washington Times*, September 25, 2001, p. A-18.

[33] Mike Tolson, "Remain objective despite war, Rather tells Texas journalists," *Houston Chronicle*, March 19, 2002, p. 19.

ists: "A journalist is never more true to democracy—is never more engaged as a citizen, is never more patriotic—than when aggressively doing the job of independently verifying the news of the day; questioning the actions of those in authority; disclosing information the public needs but others wish secret for self-interested purposes."[34] An editor at one of the top U.S. journalism reviews also implicitly endorsed patriotism in arguing that journalists serve their country best when asking "tough, even unpopular questions when our government wages war." He distinguished "patriotism, love of one's country" from "nationalism—the exalting of one's nation and its culture and interests above all others. If patriotism is a kind of affection, nationalism is its dark side."[35]

I am against nationalism, and I am against patriotism. They are both the dark side. It is time not simply to redefine a kinder-and-gentler patriotism, but to sweep away the notion and acknowledge it as morally, politically, and intellectually bankrupt. It is time to scrap patriotism.

More specifically, it is crucial to scrap patriotism in today's empire, the United States, where patriotism is not only a bad idea but literally a threat to the survival of the planet. We should abandon patriotism and strive to become more fully developed human beings not with shallow allegiances to a nation but rich and deep ties to humanity. At first glance, in a country where patriotism is almost universally taken to be an unquestioned

---

[34] Bill Kovach, "Journalism and patriotism," talk to the annual meeting of the Organization of News Ombudsmen, April 30, 2002. http://www.newsombudsmen.org/kovach.html.

[35] Russ Baker, "Want to be a patriot? Do your job," *Columbia Journalism Review*, May 2002, pp. 78–79.

virtue, this may seem outrageous. But there is a simple path to what I consider to be this simple conclusion.

What do you love?

If we use the common definition of patriotism—love of, and loyalty to, one's country—the first question that arises is, what is meant by country? Nation-states, after all, are not naturally occurring objects. What is the object of our affection and loyalty? In discussions with various community groups and classes since 9/11, I have asked people to explain which aspects of a nation-state—specifically in the context of patriotism in the United States—they believe should spark patriotic feelings. Toward whom or what should one feel love and loyalty? The answers offered include the land, the people of a nation, its culture, the leadership, national policies, the nation's institutions, and the democratic ideals of the nation. To varying degrees, all seem like plausible answers, yet all fail to provide a coherent answer to that basic question.

Land: Many people associate patriotism with a love of the land on which they were born, raised, or currently live. People's sense of place and connection to a landscape is easy to understand. Most of us have felt that, and it's a healthy instinct; it is difficult to care for something that one doesn't know well or have affection for, and we have an obligation to care for the land.

But what has that to do with love or loyalty to a nation-state? Does affection for a certain landscape map onto political boundaries? If I love the desert, should I have a greater affection for the desert on the U.S. side of the border, and a lesser affection when I cross into Mexico? Should I love the prairie in my home state of North Dakota—land where I was born and raised, and where I feel most comfortable, most at home—but abandon that affection when I hit the Canadian border? In discussing connections to the land we can talk sensibly about watersheds and local ecosystems, but not national boundaries. And ties to a specific piece of land (for example, the farm one grew up on) have nothing to do with a nation-state.

People: It's also common to talk about patriotism in terms of love and affection for one's countrywomen and men. This can proceed on two levels, either as an assertion of differential value of people's lives or as an expression of affection for people. The former—claiming that the lives of people within one's nation-state are more valuable than lives of people outside it—is unacceptable by the standards of virtually all major moral philosophies and religions, which typically are based on the belief that all human life is intrinsically equally valuable. It may be true that, especially in times of war, people act as if they believe the lives of fellow citizens are more valuable, but that cannot be a principle on which patriotism can rest.

This does not ignore the fact that we grieve differently, more intensely, when people close to us die. We feel something different over the death of someone we knew compared with the death of a stranger. But typically when we grieve more deeply for those we knew, it is because we knew them, not because we shared the same citizenship. We all have special affection for specific people in our lives, and it's likely that—by virtue of proximity—for most of us the majority of people for whom we have that affection are citizens of the same nation. But does that mean our sense of connection to them stems from living in the same nation-state and should be understood that way? Given the individual variation in humans, why assume that someone living in our nation-state should automatically spark a feeling of connection greater than someone elsewhere? I was born in the United States near the Canadian border, and I have more in common with Canadians from the prairie provinces than I do with, for example, the people of Texas, where I now live. Am I supposed to, by virtue of my U.S. citizenship, naturally feel something stronger for Texans than Manitobans? If so, why?

Culture: The same argument about land and people applies to cultures. Culture—that complex mix of language, customs, art, stories, faith, traditions—does not map exactly onto the mostly artificial boundaries of nation-states. Indeed, in many nation-states internal differences among cultures can be a source of conflict, not unity. In a society such as the United States, in which battles over these issues are routinely referred to as "the culture wars," it's difficult to imagine how patriotism could be defined as love of, or loyalty to, any particular culture or set of cultural practices.

So, if one were to proclaim that patriotism was about attachment to culture, the obvious question in a nation-state with diverse cultural groups would be, "What culture?" Up until fairly recently in U.S. history, society's answer to that, implicitly, was, "the dominant white, Anglo-American culture." We were a melting pot, but it just always seemed to turn out that the final product of the melting process didn't change much. In an era in which it is widely agreed that people have a right to maintain their particular cultural traditions, few people are going to argue that to be patriotic one must accept that long-dominant culture and abandon other traditions. And to claim that patriotism is about respect for different cultural traditions is nonsensical; respecting different cultures may be a fine principle, but it has nothing to do with love of, or loyalty to, a nation-state.

Leaders: In a democracy it should be clear that patriotism cannot be defined as loyalty to existing political leaders. Such patriotism would be the antithesis of democracy; to be a citizen is to retain the right to make judgments about leaders, not simply accept their authority. Even if one accepts the right of leaders to make decisions within a legal structure and agrees to follow the resulting laws, that does not mean one loves or is loyal to that leadership.

Policies: The same argument about leaders applies to specific policies adopted by leaders. In a democracy, one may agree to follow legally binding rules, but that does not mean one supports them. Of course, no one claims that it is unpatriotic to object to existing policy about taxes or roads or education. War tends to be the only issue about which people make demands that everyone support—or at least mute dissent about—a national policy. But why should war be different? When so much human life is at stake, is it not even more important for all opinions to be fully aired?

Governmental structures: If patriotism is not about loyalty to a particular leader or policies, many contend, at least it can mean loyalty to our governmental structures. But that is no less an abandonment of democracy, for inherent in a real democracy is the idea that no single set of institutions can be assumed to be, for all times and places, the ultimate vehicle for democracy. In a nation founded on the principle that the people are sovereign and retain the right to reject institutions that do not serve their interests, patriotism defined as loyalty to the existing structures is hard to defend.

Democratic ideals: When challenged on these other questionable definitions of the object of love or loyalty, most people eventually land on the seemingly safe assertion that patriotism in the United States is an expression of commitment to a set of basic democratic ideals, which typically include liberty, justice, and (sometimes) equality. But problems arise here as well.

First, what makes these values distinctly American? Are not various people around the world committed to these values and to working to make them real in a variety of ways? Given that these values were not invented in the United States and are not distinct to the United States today, how can one claim them as the basis for patriotism? If these values predate the formation of the United States and are present around the world, are they not human ideals rather than American?

An analogy to gender stereotypes is helpful. After 9/11, a number of commentators argued that criticisms of masculinity should be rethought. Though the hegemonic conception of masculinity is typically defined by competition, domination, and violence, they said, cannot we now see—realizing that male firefighters raced into burning buildings and risked their lives to save others—that masculinity can encompass a kind of strength that is rooted in caring and sacrifice? Of course men often exhibit such strength, just as do women. So, the obvious question arises: What makes these distinctly masculine characteristics? Are they not simply human characteristics?

We identify masculine tendencies toward competition, domination, and violence because we see patterns of differential behavior; men are more prone to such behavior in our culture. We can go on to observe and analyze the ways in which men are socialized to behave in those ways, toward the goal of changing those destructive behaviors. That analysis is different than saying that admirable human qualities present in both men and women are somehow primarily the domain of one gender. To assign them to a gender is misguided, and demeaning to the gender that is then assumed not to possess them to the same degree. Once we start saying "strength and courage are masculine traits," it leads to the conclusion that woman are not as strong or courageous. To say "strength and courage are masculine traits," then, is to be sexist.

The same holds true for patriotism. If we abandon the crude version of patriotism but try to hold onto an allegedly more sophisticated version, we bump up against this obvious question: Why are human characteristics being labeled American if there is nothing distinctly American about them?

The next move in the attempt to redeem patriotism is to claim that although these values are not the sole property of Americans, it is in the United States that they have been realized to their fullest extent. This is merely the hubris of the powerful. As discussed earlier, on some criteria—such as legal protection for freedom of speech—the United States ranks at or near the top. But the commercial media system, which dominates in the United States, also systematically shuts out radical views and narrows the political spectrum, impoverishing real democratic dialogue. It is folly to think any nation could claim to be the primary repository of any single democratic value, let alone the ideals of democracy.

Claims that the United States is the ultimate fulfillment of the values of justice also must come to terms with history and the American record of brutality, both at home and abroad. One might want to ask people of indigenous and African descent about the commitment to freedom and justice for all, in the past and today. We also would have some explaining to do to the people from nations that have been the victims of U.S. aggression, direct and indirect. Why is it that our political culture, the highest expression of the ideals of freedom and democracy, has routinely gone around the world overthrowing democratically elected governments, supporting brutal dictators, funding and training proxy terrorist armies, and unleashing brutal attacks on civilians when we go to war? If we want to make the claim that we are the fulfillment of history and the ultimate expression of the principles of freedom and justice, our first stop might be Hiroshima. Then Nagasaki.

After working through this argument in class, one student, in exasperation, told me I was missing the point by trying to reduce patriotism to an easily articulated idea or ideas. "It's about all these things together," she said. But it's not clear how individual explanations that fall short can collectively make a reasonable argument. If each attempt to articulate a basis for patriotism fails on empirical, logical, or moral grounds, how do they add up to a coherent position?

Any attempt to articulate an appropriate object of patriotic love and loyalty falls apart quickly. When I make this argument, I am often told that I simply don't understand, that patriotism is as much about feeling as it is about logic or evidence. Certainly love is a feeling that often defies exact description; when we say we love someone, we aren't expected to produce a treatise on the reasons. My point is not to suggest the emotion of love should be rendered bloodless but to point out that patriotism is incoherent because there is no object for the love that can be defended, morally or politically. We can love people, places, and ideas, but it makes no sense to declare one's love or loyalty to a nation-state that claims to be democratic.

Beyond patriotism

So, there is no way to rescue patriotism or distinguish it from nationalism, which most everyone rejects as crude and jingoistic. Any use of the concept of patriotism is bound to be chauvinistic at some level. At its worst, patriotism can lead easily to support for barbaric policies, especially in war. At its best, it is self-indulgent and arrogant in its assumptions about the uniqueness of U.S. culture and willfully ignorant about the history and contemporary policy of this country. Emma Goldman was correct when she identified the essentials of patriotism as "conceit, arrogance, and egotism" and went on to assert that:

> Patriotism assumes that our globe is divided into little spots, each one surrounded by an iron gate. Those who have had the fortune of being born on some particular spot, consider themselves better, nobler, grander, more intelligent than the living beings inhabiting any other spot. It is, therefore, the duty of everyone living on that chosen spot to fight, kill, and die in the attempt to impose his superiority upon all the others.[36]

We can retain all our affections for land, people, culture, and a sense of place without labeling it as patriotism and artificially attaching it to national boundaries. We can take into account the human need to feel solidarity and connection with others (what Randolph Bourne described as the ability "to enjoy the companionship of others, to be able to cooperate with them, and to feel a slight malaise at solitude"[37]) without attaching

---

[36] Emma Goldman, "Patriotism: A Menace to Liberty," in *Anarchism and Other Essays* (New York: Dover, 1969), pp. 128–129.

[37] Randolph Bourne, "War Is the Health of the State," 1918. http://struggle.ws/hist_texts/warhealthstate1918.html

those feelings to a nation-state. We can realize that communication and transportation technologies have made possible a new level of mobility around the world, which leaves us with a clear choice: Either the world can continue to be based on domination by powerful nation-states (in complex relationship with multinational corporations) and the elites who dictate policy in them, or we can seek a new interdependence and connection with people around the world through popular movements based on shared values and a common humanity that can cross national boundaries. To achieve the latter, people's moral reasoning must be able to constrain the destructive capacity of elite power. As Goldman suggested, patriotism retards our moral development. These are not abstract arguments about rhetoric; the stakes are painfully real and the people in subordinated nation-states have, and will continue, to pay the price of patriotism in the dominant states with their bodies.

The question of patriotism is particularly important in the United States. The greater the destructive power of a nation, the greater the potential danger of patriotism. Despite many Americans' belief that we are the first benevolent empire, this applies to the United States as clearly as to any country. On this count we would do well to ponder the observations of one of the top Nazis, Hermann Goering. In G. M. Gilbert's book on his experiences as the Nuremberg prison psychologist, he recounts this conversation with Goering:

> "Why of course the people don't want war," Goering shrugged. "Why would some poor slob on a farm want to risk his life in a war when the best that he can get out of it is to come back to his farm in one piece. Naturally, the common people don't want war; neither in Russia nor in England nor

in America, nor for that matter in Germany. That is understood. But, after all, it is the leaders of the country who determine the policy and it is always a simple matter to drag the people along, whether it is a democracy or a fascist dictatorship or a Parliament or a Communist dictatorship."

"There is one difference," I pointed out. "In a democracy the people have some say In the matter through their elected representatives, and in the United States only Congress can declare war."

"Oh, that is all well and good, but, voice or no voice, the people can always be brought to the bidding of the leaders. That is easy. All you have to do is tell them that they are being attacked and denounce the pacifists for lack of patriotism and exposing the country to danger. It works the same way in any country."[38]

If not patriotism?

An argument against patriotism raises the question of whether nation-states are a sensible way to organize our political lives. But if not the nation-state, then what? The simple answer is both the local and the global; politics must, over time, devolve down to levels where ordinary people can have a meaningful role in governing their own lives, while at the same time maintaining a sense of connection to the entire human family and understanding that the scope of high technology and the legacy of imperialism leave us bound to each other across the globe in new ways. This is a call for an internationalism that understands we live mostly at the local level but can do that ethically only when we take into account how local actions affect others outside our immediate view.

---

[38] G. M. Gilbert, *Nuremberg Diary* (New York: Farrar, Straus and Company, 1947), pp. 278–279.

My goal here is not a detailed sketch of how such a system would work. The first step is to envision something beyond what exists, a point from which people could go forward with experiments in new forms of social, political, and economic organization. Successes and failures in those experiments will guide subsequent steps, and any attempt to provide a comprehensive plan at this stage shouldn't be taken seriously. It also is important is to realize that the work of articulating alternative political visions and engaging in political action to advance them has been going on for centuries. There is no reason today to think that national identification is the only force that could hold together societies; for example, political radicals of the nineteenth and early twentieth centuries argued for recognizing other common interests. As Goldman put it:

> Thinking men and women the world over are beginning to realize that patriotism is too narrow and limited a conception to meet the necessities of our time. The centralization of power has brought into being an international feeling of solidarity among the oppressed nations of the world; a solidarity which represents a greater harmony of interests between the workingman of America and his brothers abroad than between the American miner and his exploiting compatriot; a solidarity which fears not foreign invasion, because it is bringing all the workers to the point when they will say to their masters, "Go and do your own killing. We have done it long enough for you." This solidarity is awakening the consciousness of even the soldiers, they, too, being flesh of the flesh of the great human family.[39]

---

[39] Goldman, "Patriotism," pp. 142–143.

We can, of course, go even further back in human history to find articulations of alternatives. As Leo Tolstoy reminded us in his critique of patriotism published in 1900, a rejection of loyalty to governments is part of the animating spirit of Christianity; "some 2,000 years ago . . . the person of the highest wisdom, began to recognize the higher idea of a brotherhood of man." Tolstoy argued that this "higher idea, the brotherly union of the peoples, which has long since come to life, and from all sides is calling you to itself" could lead people to "understand that they are not the sons of some fatherland or other, nor of Governments, but are sons of God."[40]

In more secular form, this sentiment is summed up often-quoted statement of the great American labor leader and socialist Eugene Debs, who said in 1915: "I have no country to fight for; my country is the earth, and I am a citizen of the world."[41]

[40] Leo Tolstoy, "Patriotism and Government," online at http://dwardmac.
pitzer.edu/Anarchist_Archives/bright/tolstoy/patriotismandgovt.html
[41] http://bari.iww.org/iu120/local/Scribner12.html

II
UNDERSTANDING POLITICAL AND INTELLECTUAL
REALITIES

AFTER 9/11, MANY Americans wanted to have a serious con-versation about the role of the United States in world affairs and its relationship to the attacks. People from a broad array of political positions were interested in a serious exploration of what had happened and why. But that kind of exploration occurred mostly at the margins. In the mainstream, such questions were largely ignored or dealt with superficially. Why was such a discussion and debate so easily derailed in a country with such expansive guarantees of political freedom, a well-developed professional journalism community, and an extensive higher-education system?

Of those questions, the most attention has been paid to journalism. There has been much criticism of the mainstream commercial news media since 9/11, some of it harsh and virtually all of it deserved.[42] In covering the aftermath of the attacks, the wars in Afghanistan and Iraq, and the ongoing "war on terror-

---

[42] For a sample of some of the best, see http://www.coldtype.net/

ism," professional journalists have failed to provide a truly independent source of factual information; the historical, political, and social context in which to make sense of those facts; and exposure to the widest range of opinion available in the society.[43] This profound failure contributed to the impoverished nature of political discourse in the United States.

Much less discussed are the general condition of our political culture and the failures of the universities. Chapter 4 looks at how ideas about the nature of democracy in the United States developed over the twentieth century, and how some of those ideas have worked against citizen engagement. Chapter 5 examines the reaction to 9/11 and the recent wars among university faculty members and suggests reasons why academia failed to provide the intellectual leadership needed to foster a healthy, functioning democracy.

---

[43] Robert Jensen, "The military's media," *The Progressive*, May 2003, pp. 22–15.

MORE FREEDOM, LESS DEMOCRACY: AMERICAN POLITICAL CULTURE IN THE TWENTIETH CENTURY

S INCE SEPTEMBER 11, 2001, I have been speaking freely in the United States, a nation whose institutions have many demo- cratic features. My free speech, which has been harshly critical of the leaders of the United States and their policies, has been dis- seminated widely through print publications, web sites, e-mail, radio, and television. Most of the exposure has been in the alter- native media, but I have appeared in mainstream channels as well. Extrapolating from the thousands of e-mail messages, let- ters, and phone calls I have received as a result of this free speech, it is reasonable to assume that tens of thousands read and take seriously my ideas, and hundreds of thousands have been exposed to those ideas in more abbreviated form via radio and television.

So, although it is true that as a political dissident I have no chance at the access to mainstream channels that "reputable" commentators can expect when they repeat the conventional wisdom, my voice did get amplified by the combination of:

— new technologies that are relatively open and have not been completely commercialized;

—a limited but active and committed alternative press;

—marginal openings in the commercial-corporate media for dissidents who have some claim to "credibility" and can provide the appearance of balance; and

—the ease with which foreign publications and web sites could pick up my work.

I have been writing in public as a journalist or scholar since my junior year in high school, and in the last three months of 2001 alone my work may well have reached more people than the total of the preceding twenty-seven years. This suggests a society that takes seriously the concept of free speech. Yet after this experience, it has never seemed clearer that free speech is fragile and democracy is in danger in the United States. This claim rests on two assertions: Meaningful free speech is about more than just the guarantee of a legal right to speak freely and the absence of governmental repression; meaningful democracy is about more than the existence of institutions that have democratic features.

To understand the state of the political culture of the United States after 9/11, it's instructive to go back to the early twentieth century and the life of one of my favorite radical Americans, Scott Nearing.

A radically good life

Nearing contended that three principles guided his life as a teacher, writer, and political activist: the quest "to learn the truth, to teach the truth, and to help build the truth into the life of the community." Nearing began his teaching career in 1906 at the University of Pennsylvania's Wharton School, where he was a popular teacher, author of widely used economics textbooks, and well-known speaker on the lecture circuit. He was on his way to a successful academic career, if not for one problem. He took seriously those three principles, and from them he formulated a simple guide to action: "If there was exploitation and corruption in the society I should speak out against it."[44]

That's when the trouble started.

By 1915 Nearing had been fired by the Penn trustees. They gave no reason publicly, but there's little doubt that his socialist views and participation in the movement to end child labor (considered a radical position at that time) played a role. Many faculty members, including some who disagreed sharply with his politics, rallied to his defense, but to no avail. Rumors of a demand made by legislators of the university's trustees—fire Nearing or lose a key appropriation—were never definitively proved, but whatever the trustees' reasons, the faculty's arguments about academic freedom did not save Nearing's job. So Nearing moved on to the University of Toledo, a public university with a broader sense of its social mission. There he quickly became an integral part of the university and community— until 1917, when he was again fired, this time for his antiwar activity.

Nearing lost his job but not his voice, and he continued his writing and political activity, including an antiwar pamphlet titled, "The Great Madness: A Victory for American Plutocracy." That landed him in federal court, one of hundreds of political dissidents tried in the World War I era under the draconian Espionage Act. Charged in 1918 with attempting to cause insubordination and mutiny and obstructing recruiting, Nearing

---

[44] Scott Nearing, *The Making of a Radical: A Political Autobiography* (White River Junction, Vermont: Chelsea Green Publishing, 2000), p. 56.

went to trial in February 1919 expecting to be convicted and ready to go to prison; sentences of five or ten years were common at the time. But he was determined to use his trial as a platform to explain his antiwar and socialist views, which he did with his usual clarity and bluntness (often, by his account, frustrating his own attorney's objections to inappropriate questions by prosecutors). His arguments from the witness stand apparently affected the jury; Nearing was found not guilty for writing the pamphlet, although the Rand School was convicted for publishing it and fined $3,000. The U.S. Supreme Court upheld what Nearing, who had a wry sense of humor, called that "unique decision." [45]

Nearing remained a popular lecturer, filling halls as large as Madison Square Garden for solo lectures and debates with Clarence Darrow and other well-known political figures, until promoters would no longer book radical speakers. When shut out of lecture halls, Nearing moved to smaller venues, including the living rooms of other radicals. He continued to write books and pamphlets, many based on his extensive travels around the world, focusing on both the corrupt nature of capitalism and imperialism, and the possibilities for a socialist future. In 1932 he turned his back on the modern economy and began a half-century of successful homesteading with his wife, Helen, first in Vermont and then in Maine. After 1917 Nearing never held a university position and was blacklisted by mainstream publishers. But he continued his writing, speaking, and activism until he died at the age of 100 in 1983. He went to his grave unwavering in his commitment to his three principles and clear that his

---

[45] Ibid., p. 117.

adherence to those principles had allowed him to live what he called simply "a good life."[46]

The expansion of free speech and the contraction of democracy

Nearing's story can help illuminate both the ways in which formal guarantees of freedom of speech and inquiry have expanded in this culture in the twentieth century and, at the same time, the ways in which American democracy has atrophied. Since Nearing was fired and hauled into court, legal protections for freedom of expression — and the culture's commitment to free speech — have become more entrenched, which is all to the good. But at the same time, the United States today is a far less vibrant political culture than it was then. This is the paradox to come to terms with: How is it that as formal freedoms that allow democratic participation have expanded, the range and importance of debate and discussion that is essential to democracy have contracted? How is it that in the United States we have arguably the most expansive free-speech rights in the industrial world and at the same time an incredibly degraded political culture? How did political freedom produce such a depoliticized culture?

First, the expansion of formal freedoms. On this front, the progress is clear. During World War I, Nearing was only one of about 2,000 people prosecuted under the Espionage Act of 1917, which was amended with even harsher provisions in 1918 by what came to be known as the Sedition Act. Hundreds went to prison. The war-related suppression of expression also was merely one component of a wave of repression — which

---

[46] Helen Nearing and Scott Nearing, *Living the Good Life* (New York: Schocken Books, 1970).

included not only prison terms but also harassment, deportation, and both state and private violence—that smashed the American labor movement and crushed radical politics. At that point in U.S. history it is fair to say that freedom of speech literally did not exist. There was no guarantee of public use of public space (such as streets or parks) for expression, and criticism of the government was routinely punished. In one of the most famous, and outrageous, cases of Nearing's time, labor leader and Socialist Party candidate Eugene Debs was forced to run his fifth and final campaign for president from a federal prison cell after he was sentenced to ten years under the Espionage Act. His crime was giving a speech which pointed out, among other things, that rich men start wars and poor men fight them.[47]

The struggle to expand the scope of freedom of expression progressed through the century, although not without setbacks. Similar harshly repressive reactions surfaced again after World War II in the twentieth century's second major Red Scare. The Supreme Court upheld the criminalization of political discourse in what became known as the Communist conspiracy cases prosecuted under the Smith Act of 1940.[48] The law made it a crime to discuss the "duty, necessity, desirability, or propriety of overthrowing or destroying the government," an odd statute in a country created by a revolution against the legal government of that day. It was not until 1957 that the Supreme Court reversed the trend in those cases, overturning convictions under the act.[49] The 1960s and 1970s brought cases that continued to

---

[47] *Debs v. United States*, 249 U.S. 211 (1919).

[48] *Dennis v. United States*, 341 U.S. 494 (1951).

[49] *Yates v. United States*, 354 U.S. 298 (1957).

make more tangible the promise of the First Amendment, including landmark decisions that made it virtually impossible for public officials to use civil libel law to punish sedition[50] and established that government could not punish incendiary speech unless it rose to the level of "incitement to imminent lawless action."[51]

This history leaves the people of the United States much freer to speak critically of government action. For example, since 9/11 many people critical of U.S. foreign and military policy have written and spoken in ways that would have without question landed them in jail in previous eras (and would land them in jail, or worse, in many other nations still today). My work in this arena has all been done while I have been a faculty member of a public university in a politically conservative state. Although there was a letter-writing campaign aimed at getting me fired and I was publicly condemned by the president of my university, there has been no serious suggestion (that I know of) by anyone in the university that I should be fired. No law enforcement agents have knocked on my door. No judge or jury has passed judgment on me. Although many readers who objected to my views have called for my firing, just as many of my critics have said they defend my right to speak even if they find what I say stupid or offensive. I have been called a lot of names, but no formal sanctions have been applied. And, more important, I have never seriously expected formal sanctions for these activities.

It is important to note that I am white and American-born, with a "normal" sounding American name (meaning, one that

---

[50] *New York Times Co. v. Sullivan*, 376 U.S. 254 (1964).
[51] *Brandenburg v. Ohio*, 395 U.S. 444 (1969).

indicates northern European roots). The hostility toward some faculty members has not stayed within such civil boundaries, most notably Sami Al-Arian, the tenured Palestinian computer science professor at the University of South Florida who was vilified in the mass media and fired in December 2001 for his political views.[52] It is likely that not only my tenured status—I can't be fired without cause, protection that few people in this economy have—but my white skin has helped protect me.

In short: I live in a society that is more tolerant of dissidents, legally and culturally, than the one in which Scott Nearing lived. For this, I am grateful. We must always remember that those expansions of our freedom to speak were not gifts from enlightened politicians and judges, but a legacy of the struggles of popular movements—socialists, labor leaders, civil-rights organizers, and antiwar demonstrators.[53] The freedom of speech we enjoy today was won by people who were despised and denigrated in their time. History has vindicated them, but in their own time they suffered greatly.

So, in many ways I am better off than Scott Nearing; it is nice to know one has a steady job and likely won't be hauled into court. But even though Nearing's speech was more constrained

---

[52] See http://w3.usf.edu/~uff/AlArian/. Al-Arian also was indicted in 2003 by the U.S. government on charges that he used an academic think-tank at USF and an Islamic charity as fronts to raise money for the Palestinian Islamic Jihad. As this book goes to press, he remains in federal custody. See http://www.amuslimvoice.org/html/sami_al-arian_s_case.html

[53] David Kairys, "Freedom of Speech," in Kairys, ed., *The Politics of Law: A Progressive Critique*, 3rd ed. (New York: Basic Books, 1998), pp. 190–215.

than mine, in some ways I envy him. That may seem odd, given that in formal terms the United States of 1919 was in many ways a much less democratic nation—not only was free speech not guaranteed but the majority of the population (women and most nonwhite citizens) were denied the right to vote. Perhaps we shouldn't call a nation a democracy when it refuses to allow the majority of adults to vote and the ultimate guardians of freedom (the Supreme Court justices) see nothing wrong with jailing a leading intellectual and presidential candidate for daring to question the judgment of his opponent.

But in another sense, the United States was a far more democratic society when Nearing took the witness stand in 1918. Many commentators have pointed out that democracy is more than the presence of certain political institutions and rules. The degree to which a society is democratic also can be judged by how extensive and active are citizens' attempts to participate in the formation of public policy. Even though marginalized and oppressed people faced more restrictions and repression in 1919, they were in many ways more active participants in democracy, engaging in political discussion and attempting to assert their rights in public.

What does democracy look like?

To make sense of all this requires a definition of democracy, which requires examination not only of the structure of the system but also of the role that people see themselves as having. One striking aspect of accounts of early twentieth century America is the vibrancy of political life then compared with today. Far more people—ordinary people, not the chattering classes—saw politics as their birthright, not as an activity limited to politicians and intellectuals. Nearing describes boisterous meetings of thousands of people who came to hear speakers and argue politics in the first decades of the century. The Red Scare of the 1910s and 1920s was designed to shut down that kind of political engagement, which was inconsistent with power's conception of democracy. One of the clearest articulations of that conception came from Walter Lippmann, a leading journalist and intellectual of the first half of the twentieth century. In a complex society, Lippmann asserted people lacked the capacity to understand public affairs well enough to take a productive role in policy formation:

> The individual man does not have opinions on all public affairs. He does not know how to direct public affairs. He does not know what is happening, why it is happening, what ought to happen. I cannot imagine how he could know, and there is not the least reason for thinking, as mystical democrats have thought, that the compounding of individual ignorances in masses of people can produce a continuous directing force in public affairs.[54]

In such elitist conceptions of democracy, the role of citizens is basically to vote—to select which group of politicians and their allied experts they would like to run the country—not to be directly involved in the formation of public policy. In Lippmann's words, "The public must be put in its place, so that it may exercise its own powers, but no less and perhaps even more, so that each of us may live free of the trampling and the roar of the bewildered herd."[55]

---

[54] Walter Lippmann, *The Phantom Public* (New York: Macmillan, 1927), p. 39.
[55] Ibid., p. 155.

Unfortunately, the herd is not only bewildered but unruly, and it keeps jumping or trampling the fence; the spirit of participatory democracy doesn't die easily. Another Red Scare was necessary in the late 1940s and 1950s. Those renewed challenges to power were beaten down by the end of the 1950s, though it turned out the politically quiescent times weren't permanent, as an expanded notion of democracy re-emerged in the civil rights, women's rights, and antiwar movements of the 1960s and 1970s. These popular struggles produced what those in power saw not as a democratic renewal but as a "crisis of democracy."

Samuel Huntington, a political scientist with solid establishment credentials, warned that the problems of governance in the United States stemmed from what he called "an excess of democracy" and the solution could be found in "a greater degree of moderation in democracy."[56] Citing universities and armies, he pointed out that not all institutions benefit from democratic structures and went on to explain that "the effective operation of a democratic political system usually requires some measure of apathy and noninvolvement on the part of some individuals and groups." Acknowledging that this "marginality" for some groups is "inherently antidemocratic," Huntington still warned against "overloading the political system with demands which extend its functions and undermine its authority." His answer: "Less marginality on the part of some groups thus needs to be replaced by more self-restraint on the part of all groups."[57]

---

[56] Samuel P. Huntington, "The United States," in Michel Crozier, et al., *The Crisis of Democracy* (New York: New York University Press, 1975), p. 113.

[57] Ibid., p. 114.

In the real world, it usually turns out that restraint is expected from the "special interests" (defined as organized labor, students, women, minority groups, farmers—in other words, the vast majority of the population) to make sure there are no restraints on the "national interest" (corporate shareholders, the managerial class, defense contractors, the generals). One might reasonably ask how this promotes democracy, but from the point of view of elites Huntington's assessment is correct. If one is concerned about "governability," defined as the ability of elites to make decisions unimpeded by the people, then the excesses of democracy that come with strong popular movements are indeed the heart of the crisis.

But, of course, there are other conceptions of the role of people in democracy. Political scientist C. Douglas Lummis suggests that "there is democracy where the people have the power." But how to understand what is meant by "the people" and "the power"? For Lummis:

> [D]emocracy is not the name of any particular arrangement of political or economic institutions. Rather, it is a situation that political or economic institutions may or may not help to bring about. It describes an ideal, not a method for achieving it. It is not a kind of government, but an end of government; not a historically existing institution, but a historical project.[58]

If that is true, then one would not speak of living in a democracy, but instead speak of the degree to which different features and processes of a society are democratic—or, even more precisely, the degree to which those features and processes foster

---

[58] C. Douglas Lummis, *Radical Democracy* (Ithaca, NY: Cornell University Press, 1996), p. 22.

democracy. That includes an assessment of the democratic character not only of governmental institutions but all institutions, private and public. It is in this sense that Scott Nearing lived in a more democratic America. Even though they faced more governmental impediments to exercising power, average people of that time were more actively engaged in political dialogue, in political life.

American propaganda

After 9/11, my writing found wide distribution through a number of web sites and e-mail lists. I also wrote some pieces specifically for mainstream media outlets, though it was difficult to break into those pages. Because of the efforts of two progressive media projects that work to get critical analysis on the air and in the news (Mainstream Media Project[59] and Institute for Public Accuracy[60]), I also appeared on about eighty radio shows in the three months after the attacks—everything from a Canadian Broadcasting Company debate with a prowar conservative, to interviews with DJs at commercial stations who weren't quite sure what to make of me, to sympathetic discussions with progressive hosts on community radio stations.

So, my concern is not that I, and people with similar views, was not heard. The problem was that I was writing, speaking, and being heard in a context for political action that was much different than in Nearing's time. Although more people could hear me, being heard had a far more limited effect, not only on the immediate question of the war but more generally on the political culture. When Nearing spoke, he spoke to audiences in

---

[59] http://www.mainstream-media.net/
[60] http://www.accuracy.org/

which a high percentage of people believed that political activity by people organized into mass movements could make a difference. Much of this was no doubt rooted in an understanding of the class divisions that structured American society, and the relationship of that structure to questions of war and imperialism.

There are people in the United States today interested in building a mass movement around these issues. However, many people — even many left/progressive people — do not believe there is any meaningful channel for action. Based on thousands of conversations and correspondences with such folks, it is my experience that many do not belong to political organizations or are not active in political organizations. Given that social change in the history of this country has been largely the result of popular movements putting pressure on elites to enact progressive policies, the relative absence of such collective action is troubling. It does not mean no other possible avenues for social change exist apart from mass movements (though I can't imagine what they might be), but we should not be optimistic about alternatives without evidence. I have yet to hear any strategy for change that leads me to believe that mass movements are now irrelevant.

This state of affairs is not accidental. As the late sociologist Alex Carey puts it, "The twentieth century has been characterized by three developments of great political importance: the growth of democracy, the growth of corporate power, and the growth of corporate propaganda as a means of protecting corporate power against democracy."[61] I would add to that the

---

[61] Alex Carey, *Taking the Risk out of Democracy: Corporate Propaganda versus Freedom and Liberty* (Urbana: University of Illinois Press, 1997), p. 18.

development of propaganda to protect state power, which is tightly interwoven with corporate power. Carey's point is that people with power have been engaged in pacifying the population through propaganda to make sure the expansion of formal democracy—through greater expression and organizing rights, and an expanded franchise—does not result in a real democratization of the society, especially the economy.

Edward Bernays, often described as the father of the public relations industry, explained—from a celebratory point of view—how propaganda is "the executive arm of the invisible government."[62] Who are those "invisible governors"? Those with "qualities of natural leadership" who "supply needed ideas" and hold "a key position in the social structure."[63] The opening lines of his 1928 book *Propaganda* make clear how the system works:

> The conscious and intelligent manipulation of the organized habits and opinions of the masses is an important element in democratic society. Those who manipulate this unseen mechanism of society constitute an invisible government which is the true ruling power of our country. We are governed, our minds our molded, our tastes formed, our ideas suggested, largely by men we have never heard of. This is a logical result of the way in which our democratic society is organized.[64]

Bernays acknowledged that some aspects of the propaganda process—"the manipulation of news, the inflation of personal-

---

[62] Edward L. Bernays, *Propaganda* (New York: Horace Liverright, 1928), p. 20.

[63] Ibid., p. 9.

[64] Ibid.

ity, the general ballyhoo by which politicians and commercial products and social ideas are brought to the consciousness of the masses"—are often criticized and can be misused. "But such organization and focusing are necessary to orderly life."[65]

From a more critical view, Carey described this same propaganda project as "a 75-year-long multi-billion dollar project in social engineering on a national scale." Carey's study of the propaganda campaign suggests that starting in the 1930s American business leaders realized that they could not keep labor subjugated indefinitely through brute force. So, they turned to "a competition for public opinion via the mass media."[66] Carey's account of the operations of such groups as the National Association of Manufacturers shows how corporate leaders used advertising, public relations, media relations, and their influence on the educational system to deal with threats to their power.

In addition to campaigns for specific policies, there have been two key underlying messages to this propaganda in the past half-century. First, not only is capitalism the natural economic system and the only one compatible with democracy, but unions and other vehicles for popular organizing somehow disrupt what would be an otherwise harmonious system in which benevolent owners and hardworking managers labor selflessly to provide for customers and workers. Second, the United States is unique among world governments, past and present, in its pursuit of democracy and freedom in the world. While other nations act out of self-interest, the United States goes forward with a benevolent mission.

---

[65] Ibid., p. 12.
[66] Carey, p. 20.

The system that propagates these fictions is happy to concede that sometimes corporations do unpleasant things and sometimes the government makes mistakes—usually the result of the bad behavior of individuals. If the problems seem to go beyond individuals, we are assured that the miraculous workings of the market and democracy have corrected the problems and produced a "change of course" for the institutions involved. Unlike more totalitarian systems, this arrangement is flexible and better able to adapt to public pressure: absorbing and co-opting dissent when possible, coercing through relatively subtle methods when necessary, resorting to force and violence only when other methods have failed.

The effects of this relentless propaganda are clear. Many people accept the mythology, even when it is directly contradicted by their own experience. But more important, many of those who reject the mythology do not contest the naturalizing of the underlying system of domination, or can't imagine how to contest it. After public talks about corporate domination or American imperialism, I get two common responses. One is a judgment rooted in the condescension of the comfortable: "Well, you are right, but there's nothing anyone can do about it—people don't want (or are too stupid) to change." The other is a question framed by despair and isolation: "Is there anything I can do?"

The answer to the first is simple: There is nothing in human history that leads to the conclusion that people inherently crave subordination or cannot find ways to resist it. The response to the second is equally simple: Organize, become part of a movement. There is always something that can be done, but it must be done through collective action, and it will take time; entrenched systems of power don't go away overnight. The details of what to do are not quite so easy to work out, but it is clear they must be worked out with other people, not on one's own.

Those two questions sum up my point about the more democratic spirit of Scott Nearing's times. People in Nearing's audiences did not need to be told that humans were capable of independent thought and action. People did not have to be told that resisting concentrations of power required organizing. The political climate of the time took those as givens. That doesn't mean that every single person believed in the power or wisdom of participatory democracy and mass movements, but simply that there was a more hospitable context for people to act. Nearing's words were spoken to a more politically engaged culture. The words of contemporary antiwar activists after 9/11 were spoken to a world in which none of those things could be taken for granted.

Given the contingencies of history and the difficulty in predicting the course of politics, definitive judgments are difficult to make. But based on my experience, I believe that even though my work may be read and heard by more people than Scott Nearing's, it has far less impact. In a society in which free speech is in some sense irrelevant, public political life is little more than a sideshow. And if public political life is a sideshow, what do we say about the state of our democracy?

Beyond parody

Our current situation constitutes a "crisis of democracy," understood not in Huntington's terms but in the sense used by legal scholar David Kairys in this summary of U.S. political life:

> [D]espite all the rhetoric about free speech and our democratic political process, a very large proportion of us—perhaps

most—feel silenced and disenfranchised. There is a widespread recognition across the political spectrum that the American people lack the effective means to be heard or to translate their wishes into reality through the political process. There is, and has been for some time, a crisis of democracy and freedom that has been ignored by public officials and the media.[67]

My only dispute with Kairys's claim is the last sentence; I am not so sure this crisis has been ignored by public officials or the media. Rather, it is a state of affairs with which most public officials and the media are perfectly content because, no matter what the rhetoric, those centers of power either believe Lippmann was right or, in the case of the more crass, know Lippmann was wrong but find his conception of democracy useful in taming the "bewildered herd." But if Kairys means there is a deeper crisis that even the officials don't understand, a crisis of legitimacy, he may be right.

A few years ago I would have argued that the struggle for the soul of the nation was between radical democrats such as Lummis, who believe that the role of citizens in democracy should be as full participants, and elitist theorists of democracy such as Lippmann, who believe that such participatory ideals are not feasible and that a citizen's job is to ratify the decisions of experts and professional politicians through regular voting. My view is that in a meaningful democratic system, citizens should not be limited only to selecting leaders (an incredibly thin conception of democracy) or to selecting policies from a set of limited choices presented to them by leaders (still a thin con-

---

[67] Kairys, p. 11.

ception). In a democratic system with a rich sense of participation, citizens would play an active, meaningful role in determining which issues are most important at any moment and forming policy options to address those issues.

Today, we may be moving to a society in which even Lippmann's impoverished notion of democracy seems idealistic, as the quality of public discourse continues to degrade. We live in an era in which policy proposals are treated not as topics for discussion by the people but products to be sold to them. Forget democracy-as-participation. Even democracy-as-ratification is unrealistic. Today, we have democracy-as-stupefaction. The goal of politicians and their consultants seems to be to stupefy, to dull the faculties of people, just as product advertising leaves people stupefied. To borrow from the dictionary definition, politics seems to be designed to leave people in "a state of suspended or deadened sensibility."

How else to describe a situation in which the Bush administration can appoint an advertising executive to be Under Secretary of State for Public Diplomacy and Public Affairs, charged with the task of "selling" U.S. policy to the Muslim world? Charlotte Beers's fitness for the job could be seen in her previous successes—Uncle Ben's rice ("Perfect every time"), Head and Shoulders shampoo ("Helps bring you closer"), and American Express ("Don't leave home without it").[68] Secretary of State Colin Powell—Beers's boss until her resignation in March 2003—explained that the new focus of public diplomacy would be "really branding foreign policy, branding the depart-

---

[68] Martin Fletcher, "Publicity queen sells America to the Muslims," *Times of London*, October 16, 2001, p. 3.

ment, marketing the department, marketing American values to the world and not just putting out pamphlets."[69]

When asked why the Bush administration waited until after Labor Day to launch its campaign to convince the American public that military action against Iraq was necessary, White House Chief of Staff Andrew Card said, "From a marketing point of view, you don't introduce new products in August."[70] When that war was over (or, at least, at the end of "major combat operations," as the president put it on May 1, 2003), the White House created the ultimate campaign photo — the president bounding out of a jet plane that had just landed on an aircraft carrier, dressed in a flight suit with a pilot's helmet tucked under his arm, flashing a cocky *Top Gun* grin. Although a few Democrats criticized such a cynical use of the war for political purposes ("I am loathe to think of an aircraft carrier being used as an advertising backdrop for a presidential political slogan, and yet that is what I saw," said West Virginia senator Robert Byrd[71]) the photo of the beaming president was on the front page of virtually every American newspaper the next morning. When the war dragged on and the "Mission Accomplished" backdrop from the aircraft carrier speech became a bit embarrassing, the White House had a solution — fly Bush into Baghdad for two-and-a-half hours on the ground to allow photographers to snap pictures of him serving Thanksgiving dinner

---

[69] Colin Powell, testimony to House Budget Committee, March 15, 2001.

[70] Elisabeth Bumiller, "Traces of terror: The strategy; Bush aides set strategy to sell policy on Iraq," *New York Times*, September 7, 2002, p. A1.

[71] Ken Guggenheim, "Byrd rips Bush's aircraft carrier use," Associated Press, May 6, 2003.

to the troops. The next day, there on the front page of America's newspapers, was the president gripping a tray with a big, plump turkey, boosting the morale of the troops. As in advertising, when one image gets stale, it can simply be replaced.

Of course politicians and policies have been sold like products before. But these post-9/11 tactics were not only openly discussed without shame, but with some pride, either to indicate how forward-thinking the administration was to realize it must win the hearts and minds in the world of Islam or to indicate how politically savvy this administration is. Such a state of affairs is beyond parody. But it is not beyond hope.

There is no reason to think that a revitalization of radical democracy is impossible. There is no reason to think that we are on the other side of some fault line in human history that makes collective action no longer relevant. Certain institutions in our society—a media not controlled directly by the state, and higher education—have democratic features that can be used to fight concentrations of illegitimate authority. The first step in understanding how to use those institutions is to understand how they have failed us so far.

KNOWING AND DOING:
THE FAILURES OF THE UNIVERSITY

IN 1979 I worked as a busboy in a restaurant in one of the Washington, D.C., suburbs, where I became friends with one of the dishwashers, who was Middle Eastern. On one slow night when I first got to know him, we sat for a long time talking, and I asked him what country he was from. "Persia," he said. I looked at him, confused. "I don't understand," I said. "Persia isn't a country anymore." He smiled and explained. He was Iranian. But this was after the fall of the Shah, when Americans from the U.S. embassy in Tehran were being held in the infamous "hostage crisis." All over the United States, Iranians and Iranian-Americans were subject to both verbal and physical abuse. My restaurant friend explained that to avoid such abuse, he simply told Americans he was from Persia, and that took care of it. He said he felt bad about fudging his own nationality, but he was scared for his safety.

At the time, I was a temporary college dropout, with no particular expertise in the Middle East. But from reading the papers and my dim memories of world history class, I knew that modern-day Iran had taken the place of what had been called Persia.

I couldn't have told anyone much about the history of the Persian Empire or contemporary Iranian politics, beyond what was in the news at the time. But I had assumed everyone knew at least as much as I knew, which wasn't much. I asked him how he could fool people simply by calling himself Persian. He smiled.

"I don't mean to sound rude," he said. "But it's easy to fool Americans."

The eggshell of ignorance

The Buddha is said to have spoken of enlightenment as emerging from the eggshell of ignorance. The events of 9/11 shattered our eggshell and presented Americans with a stark choice. For too long we had lived with a willed ignorance about the consequences of U.S. economic, foreign, and military policy that to many felt like protection from the world — on the absurd assumption that what we don't know can't hurt us — but in reality was always eggshell-thin.

This ignorance was perhaps most clearly expressed by the president of the United States. At an October 11, 2001, news conference, Bush told reporters he was amazed by what he called the "vitriolic hatred for America" in some Islamic countries. He explained:

> I'm amazed that there is such misunderstanding of what our country is about, that people would hate us. I am, I am— like most Americans, I just can't believe it. Because I know how good we are, and we've go to do a better job of making our case. We've got to do a better job of explaining to the people in the Middle East, for example, that we don't fight a war against Islam or Muslims. We don't hold any religion accountable. We're fighting evil. And these murderers have

hijacked a great religion in order to justify their evil deeds. And we cannot let it stand.[72]

We should give the American public the benefit of the doubt and assume that most were not quite as amazed as the president. But Bush was not the only American who was inside the eggshell on September 10, 2001. On September 11, we had the opportunity to emerge, newly engaged in honest attempts to understand the world and our place in it. But many Americans desperately tried to paste the old eggshell back together. On this front, Bush also took the lead. On September 27, 2001, Bush appeared at O'Hare Airport in Chicago and encouraged people to "get on board," but not with a serious plan for educating ourselves. His advice:

> When they struck, they wanted to create an atmosphere of fear. And one of the great goals of this nation's war is to restore public confidence in the airline industry. It's to tell the traveling public: Get on board. Do your business around the country. Fly and enjoy America's great destination spots. Get down to Disney World in Florida. Take your families and enjoy life, the way we want it to be enjoyed.[73]

So, a president who claims not to understand what is obvious to virtually everyone outside the United States—that no matter what the twisted theology and ideology of Al-Qaeda, lots of

---

[72] George W. Bush, White House news conference, October 11, 2001. Text available at http://www.whitehouse.gov/news/releases/2001/10/20011011-7-index.html

[73] George W. Bush, O'Hare International Airport, Chicago, September 27, 2001. Text available at http://www.whitehouse.gov/news/releases/2001/09/20010927-1.html

people in the Arab and Muslim world object to U.S. foreign policy for perfectly rational reasons—suggests the appropriate responses are to: Explain to people in the Middle East why they don't understand American benevolence, and explain to people in the United States that they should go to Disney World, a fantasy park where one can ignore reality.

The United States is a society in which people not only can get by without knowing much about the wider world but are systematically encouraged not to think independently or critically and instead to accept the mythology of the United States as a benevolent, misunderstood giant as it lumbers around the world trying to do good. That means the crisis in which we find ourselves after 9/11 is not only political but intellectual, a problem not just of doing but of knowing.

Institutional accountability

Part of the responsibility for this failure of knowing in American culture lies with the universities. This was true before 9/11, and even more obvious after that day. Much to my sadness, U.S. faculty members—conservative and liberal alike—have for the most part either actively encouraged the avoidance of unpleasant realities or failed to fulfill their obligation to guide people toward the knowledge that would help deconstruct American mythology. This becomes clear when we look at the main responses to 9/11 in the intellectual world. There were five basic positions staked out:

1. The Ultra-Hawks: These people started with the assumption that we had to respond to the attacks of 9/11 with massive military force, arguing that the United States is the benevolent empire and the empire should do its work. If you disagreed with that, you were a fool, a dupe, or subversive.

2. The Hawks: This group conceded that there could be a debate about war, so long as that debate distorted, trivialized, and marginalized arguments against war. There was no need to analyze the situation beyond clichés about "Islamic fascism" and the assertion that the power to bomb = the right to bomb = the inevitability of bombing = the nobility of bombing. After this pseudo-debate was over (quickly), the only possible path was war.

3. The Cultural Doves: The focus of this group was the need to understand other cultures, while avoiding the crucial political issues and abstaining from debate about war.

4. The Political Doves-with-Wings-Pinned: These folks generally said that bombing is bad policy but largely avoided doing anything to press that point or to confront directly the mythology of the culture, lest they offend, because offending people is bad.

5. The Anti-Empire Crowd: People critiquing American foreign policy and militarism from an internationalist perspective rejected claims about American exceptionalism, and engaged in public education and political organizing.

From that construction it is obvious I put myself in the latter category (with the implication, of course, that it is the appropriate analysis and strategy). But here I am more interested in what we can learn about American intellectuals from the other four categories.

In certain intellectual and political circles, it is easy to criticize the Ultra-Hawks; their demand for a reflexive subordination to political leaders is a profoundly anti-intellectual position that inhibits meaningful attempts at critical thinking and democracy, which are inextricably linked. The Hawks are marginally more sophisticated in their approach, realizing that crude nationalism is not always effective. But in the end, there is little meaningful difference between the Ultra and Regular-Strength Hawks. Both groups ignore evidence and arguments that undermine their positions because the realities of power allow them to do so.

I suspect that is why, a few weeks after 9/11, a Canadian Broadcasting Corp. radio producer who wanted to set up a debate between the anti- and pro-war positions called saying she might have to cancel the segment because she couldn't find a pro-war faculty member in the United States to debate me on the air. I was incredulous, and told her that I couldn't believe people were afraid of debating me (I'm not that formidable or well known). She agreed, and said it had nothing to do with me. The pro-war folks she had talked to simply said they weren't interested in a debate, with anyone. Most likely, their refusal was based on the assessment that they had already won. Why get mixed up in a public debate in which you would have to defend your views when your views have already prevailed?

But, for all the obvious problems in these Hawk positions (assuming one believes that facts matter in determining a course of action and that moral considerations are relevant to policy discussions), one often can learn more from looking closely at the positions of what, at first glance, appear to be one's allies. I do not take this to be a case of petty backbiting, but rather important to an examination of fundamental flaws in U.S. intellectual and political culture. My target is not a specific political position, but the way in which U.S. intellectuals have contributed to the depoliticization of the culture more generally.

The Cultural Doves are well intentioned, which usually makes them dangerous. For example, after 9/11, many non-Muslims rushed to stores to buy books on Islam. There's nothing wrong with wanting to know more about Islam, and a complete understanding of what happened on 9/11 involves some knowledge of Islam. But far more important for most Americans is expanding their knowledge about U.S. foreign policy. That is, 9/11 involved theology, but it was primarily a political event, not a religious one. This tendency in the United States to want to explain things in cultural, not political, terms is dangerous in an already deeply depoliticized society.

We should never expect much, in terms of analysis or political action, from the Cultural Doves. I want to concentrate on the Political Doves-with-Wings-Pinned and try to bring into sharp focus some of the current intellectual and political problems I see. To do this, I'm going to quote extensively from an e-mail exchange I had with a fellow professor—whom I'll call John here—at the University of Texas. John has always been thoughtful and engaged in his interactions with me and has tried, in his own way, to be supportive of my political work. He makes his own attempts at sharing his views with the public through op/ed writing, which I support, even though I rarely agree with the approach he takes in his writing. He is a serious scholar in his field, and I have no reason to think he is not a principled person. But even with all those endorsements, I think his approach to politics—and the connection between professional intellectuals and politics—exemplifies some of what is wrong with the U.S. academy.

The importance of engaging

This exchange started after I had been publicly condemned by the president of the University of Texas for writing articles critical of the mad rush to war after 9/11 (see Introduction). John was critical of the president's actions and of me, and I tried to answer his points and explain my decisions.

First, he thought it untoward of me to "act as if your piece was reasonable and inoffensive." The marriage of the two descriptions implies that reasoned arguments should be inoffensive. I think my writing was, and continues to be, reasonable — that is, I present accurate factual evidence, rational arguments, and a defensible conclusion. I also understand that it offends many people. It is hardly surprising that some very reasonable presentations are also very offensive to some. Anyone who has ever taught material that deals with political and social issues knows, for example, that students who hear a point of view that contradicts what they have long been taught may well be offended; it's sometimes a sign that learning is taking place.

John also suggested that I had "initiated an inflammatory argument" with my article, which I think gets the sequence of events wrong. As I pointed out in the Introduction, the hawkish and inflammatory rhetoric of the Bush administration, members of Congress (both Republican and Democrat), TV anchors, pundits, and many others within the first hours after the attack "initiated" the argument and made it necessary for people with antiwar politics to respond immediately and decisively. I explained to John that I knew perfectly well that the piece I wrote would anger the majority of Americans. I pointed out that my goal at that moment was not to convince everyone that a war would be wrong; I knew that would be impossible. My goal was to reach out to progressive people who might be struggling for a way to understand the events of the day, to give them an analysis that would be otherwise hard to find in the mass media, to let them know they weren't alone. My e-mail traffic in the days and months after 9/11 suggests that I — and many others writing and speaking in similar fashion—accomplished that. To do that, however, I knew many people would be angry with me.

John's response to this was to point out that I had admitted I "did not care about how the majority of people would react." Indeed, I not only knew many would be angry, but I didn't care, in moral terms. (I cared in strategic terms, but made a judgment that the goal of reaching one segment of the U.S. public outweighed the effects of angering another segment.) I didn't care then, and I don't care now, because I believed—and continue to believe—that the lives of people outside the United States who would be targeted in a U.S. war were more important than the feelings of people in the United States. My intention was to help build an antiwar movement that could derail the expected U.S. military response. If a successful movement could help save innocent lives, would that not trump concerns about offending or angering some Americans? In fact, would not one be morally obligated to offend Americans?

I am not succumbing to delusional self-aggrandizement. I did not somehow think my op/eds, radio interviews, or public talks would turn the tide, and I was not naive about the chances of stopping the U.S. attack on Afghanistan. But, whatever the chances, the calculation that many in the antiwar movement made seems to me, in retrospect, to have been correct. One could argue that a less confrontational strategy could have been more effective—though I don't see any evidence for that—but that's a tactical issue, not a question of principle.

But here is the most distressing thing John said to me:

"All I can say, Bob, AGAIN is that I am glad for you that you can view the world in such black and white terms, a world where Bob Jensen carries and promotes truth and virtue, and those who react to the things he does should be judged without considering what he has done to provoke such reactions, or what he might have done to make the outcome different."

As I have explained, I did consider the reactions my work could be expected to provoke, and I judged the negative reactions to be less important than what I believed, and still believe, to be a compelling political goal that easily outweighs offending some. But the distressing part of that paragraph to me is that John seems to take refuge in—and implicitly makes a virtue out of—what he describes as an inability or unwillingness to form a clear conclusion on which one could act, and denigrating my attempt to do that. In his formulation, I am reduced to a simplistic thinker who can see only black and white, apparently less virtuous than those who see the many shades of gray.

I have never claimed to be a big thinker or an important theorist. I think I have a fairly accurate and healthy intellectual self-image: I am a competent, hard-working second-tier intellectual. I have never broken new ground, but I can do reasonably decent work building on the insights of others. I am far from the most sophisticated thinker in the world, but I think I have mastered the basics of informal logic and argumentation. And, I realize the world is a complex place. But no matter what the complexity of the world, we have moral obligations that don't go away simply because we might be less than absolutely certain about causes and consequences of actions in that complex world. One of the tasks of an intellectual should be to look for patterns in the world's complexity that can guide us in making moral and political decisions. The importance of that task increases dramatically when one lives in the most powerful country in the history of the planet, a country in which leaders have demonstrated repeatedly a willingness to use horrific levels of violence to impose their will on others.

I do not see the world in black and white. The shades of gray bedevil me as much as the next person. Like most people, I live with high levels of self-doubt. But I do not think those shadings absolve me of my responsibility. We should approach that responsibility with great humility and openness to counterarguments. We should always keep in mind that we act with imperfect knowledge; history reminds us that no small number of people who acted out of certainty about the accuracy of their analysis and the righteousness of their moral stance have brought upon the innocents of the world suffering beyond description.

But it is also true that I live in a country that drops cluster bombs in civilian areas. I have never lived anywhere that was the target of a cluster bomb, but I suspect that when a cluster bomb detonates above a person and its couple of hundred individual bomblets are dispersed to do their flesh-shredding work, the world looks pretty black and white. (More on cluster bombs in Chapter 6.) I suspect that when one sees a child pick up an unexploded bomblet from a cluster bomb, which then explodes and rips off the child's head, the world looks pretty black and white. Should the world look any less black and white when one lives in the country that drops those bombs? When the chairman of the Joint Chiefs of Staff explains, in response to a question of why such a weapon is used, that "We only use cluster munitions when they are the most effective weapon for the intended target,"[74] how long can we allow ourselves to paint pictures with the many shades of gray?

---

[74] "DoD News Briefing—Secretary Donald Rumsfeld and General Richard Myers," U.S. Department of Defense News Transcript, October 25, 2001. http://usinfo.state.gov/regional/nea/sasia/afghan/text2001/1026dod.htm.

What a healthy intellectual community would look like

Right after 9/11 there was a spate of stories about the pressures faced by faculty members who didn't fall in line behind the so-called war on terrorism. But, with rare exceptions, those pressures were informal or social, not formal or legal. For example, I know of no direct action taken by administrators at the University of Texas, where I work, to silence dissent.

But my critique of universities is not that administrators routinely persecuted dissidents, just as my criticism of most academics is not that they should be condemned because they didn't agree with me. Instead, the fundamental failure of U.S. universities after 9/11 was the unwillingness to take seriously their role as centers of knowledge and their refusal to create space for debate and discussion. If American campuses were healthy intellectual communities, after 9/11 they would have been hotbeds of discussion.

People often ask me, what would you have done if you had been president of your university? The answer is simple: After 9/11 I would have reserved the largest hall on campus for a weekly series of programs on terrorism and American foreign policy, drawing on the expertise of the campus from as many perspectives as possible. I would have committed resources from my office to publicize the forums as widely as possible. I would have made it clear that the university saw the enhancement of public discussion as central to its mission. I would have explained that although the university as an institution would take no specific position on policy choices, it would facilitate the broadest and deepest discussion possible. I would have asked my staff to work with the local television and radio stations, especially cable-access TV and community radio, to broadcast these forums. And I would have encouraged faculty members to take up these issues in the classroom when relevant.

In short, I would have taken seriously the notion that the university is a place where citizens could expect to find information, analysis, and engagement. I would have realized that at such a pivotal moment in the nation's history, the university had a unique role to play. But the University of Texas did none of that, nor did most universities in the United States. At some universities, small groups of faculty who were concerned about the direction the country was heading did their best to create such space. But on most campuses, a tiny minority of faculty was involved in such efforts, and an even smaller minority of administrators aided them. Many of the events on campuses were student-organized, efforts that were important and admirable. But it's a shame that, in most cases, university offi cials and faculty members chose to duck and cover.

A problem of the university, and beyond

Why would the largest university in the country, with such tremendous human and material resources, be so politically flat at such a crucial time? No doubt part of the explanation for the timid performance of the University of Texas, and institutions of higher education more generally, is specific to that moment. The United States had never experienced an attack on its civil ian population of that magnitude, and it's easy to understand why many people lost their voices in the highly emotional, hyper-patriotic fervor that followed. But college campuses have not been centers of critical inquiry in some time (and even when they were, such as in the 1960s, much of the most vibrant intellectual and political activity was student-led). While not pretending there was ever in the United States a golden age in which universities were completely free spaces, no doubt part of the explanation for this consistent failure is intensifying economic pressures, as public universities are forced to find more and more funding from private sources and an ethic of public service continues to wither.[75] Faculty feel this pressure, which subtly encourages professors to act not as members of a community of scholars with obligations to the public but as independent agents with the goal of maximizing grant funding and personal status. The market model dominates not only the organization of the institution but the mission as well, as students increasingly look at a university education not as an opportunity for intellectual enrichment but a ticket to upward mobility and career advancement.

But there also is a larger lesson about the culture in all of this. I quoted extensively from my exchange with John because he is one of the professors on campus who routinely offers his views on matters of public concern in public. He and I agree that academics should be part of the political dialogue, not just in the classroom or with scholarly colleagues, but in the larger world as well. But also in his comments are, I believe, strains of a view common in the United States: If one talks politics, one should make sure no one is offended. The often-repeated advice is that it's best to avoid talking politics or religion at the dinner table (or, more generally, at social gatherings), but I think that doesn't capture the real rule in the contemporary United States: One

---

[75] Lawrence C. Soley, *Leasing the Ivory Tower : The Corporate Takeover of Academia* (Boston: South End Press, 1995); George Monbiot, *Captive State: The Corporate Takeover of Britain* (London: Macmillan, 2000), Chapter 9, "Silent Science — The Corporate Takeover of the Universities."

may talk politics or religion, as long as it doesn't upset anyone. In my limited travels abroad and extensive discussions with people from other countries, this appears to be peculiar to Americans (and especially to white middle-class Americans).

At the heart of this play-nice/avoid-conflict/make-sure-no-one-feels-uncomfortable style is an implicit abandonment both of intellectual standards and political life. If we can't engage each other, and take the chance that tempers might flare, then we will be less likely to subject each other's arguments to critical scrutiny. And if we don't routinely engage in those kinds of exchanges, the skills of argumentation and informal logic—the ability to identify the logical path of a claim and evaluate the evidence—will atrophy. Yes, it's true that political debate sometimes descends into name-calling and emotional outbursts that can be destructive or even abusive. But that's all the more reason for those who have claims based in logic and evidence to be willing to debate—with passion—those claims. If argumentation (of the rigorous kind) is not going to degrade into mere argument (of the inane kind), we all have to be willing to engage with each other.

That problem did not begin on 9/11. Here's an earlier example: When the U.S. attack on Yugoslavia began in 1999, I posted a message to a progressive faculty e-mail list about a local demonstration against the bombing. One member of the list responded, asking if this were perhaps a case where progressive people should be supporting a U.S. war. Because I knew a lot of folks were buying Clinton's "humanitarian intervention" argument, I wrote a response that explained why I believed that U.S. actions were humanitarian neither in motivation nor effect, and why one should oppose the policy as immoral and illegal. My response politely but firmly put forward a political argument, not a personal attack; I made no reference to the person who had written, only to the political position she had articulated. But another list member posted a note accusing me of just such a personal attack and cautioning against such posts. I was a bit taken aback; even in allegedly left circles, and among other university faculty, I was being chastised for arguing forcefully for a position, if someone else in the group took a different position. One other person on the e-mail list defended the need for such exchanges of views, but the list generally fell silent, rendering useless a possible site for discussion and organizing. I have no idea what kept people from talking or getting involved, though I assumed part of the answer was a fear of venturing into territory where there would be sharp disagreement.

Is it too much to ask that people—especially faculty at a public university—be willing to engage in the spirited intellectual and political exchanges, which should be the life-blood of a healthy democracy? We cannot simply blame politicians or loud-mouthed TV talk show hosts for the sad state of our political culture and feel absolved. We have to take responsibility ourselves, the focus of the next section.

III
CONFRONTING OURSELVES

T HERE IS ALWAYS a personal and emotional dimension to politics. When we try to understand and analyze systems and structures of power, we quickly realize that they affect us down to the level of our daily lives, for better or worse depending on our location in those systems and structures. But the more affluent the society, the easier it is to ignore that basic fact.

This section looks at some of the crucial issues that arise when we take seriously the connection between the personal and political in the context of being citizens of a nation seeking global dominance, citizens of the empire. The final two chapters are, in some sense, discussions of personal responsibility. Because reactionary right-wing forces have used the notion of personal responsibility as a weapon against poor and oppressed people— suggesting that it is entirely one's own fault if one isn't successful in our society—progressive people sometimes shy away from these issues. But, in fact, it is affluent people who face the most difficult questions about personal responsibility. Although it's true that we live within systems we didn't choose and are struggling to change, we still face choices in our daily lives about how we will confront those systems. In many ways, this is one of the most difficult aspects of politics in an affluent society.

Chapter 6 directly engages those questions about our own lifestyles and their relationship to the empire. Chapter 7 wrestles with the problem of despair and suggests reasons we should be hopeful about the possibilities, personal and political.

SEEKING PAIN AND REDUCING PLEASURE

I N MOST SITUATIONS, people tend to seek pleasure and avoid
pain. But at this moment in history, U.S. citizens need to
invert that. If we want to become human beings in the fullest
sense of the term, if we want to be something more than comfortable and complacent citizens of the empire, then we have to
start seeking pain and reducing our pleasure.

That doesn't mean we must become masochists who live in
denial of the joy of living. Rather, it suggests that to be fully alive
we must stop turning away from a certain kind of pain and start
questioning a certain kind of pleasure. I mean this quite literally,
and with a sense of urgency; the survival of the species and the
planet may well depend on Americans becoming pain-seeking
and pleasure-reducing folks.

Conversations I had with two students several months after
9/11 help explain what this means. One young woman came to
my office the day after we had watched a documentary in class
about the 1991 Gulf War and its devastatingly brutal effects—
immediate and lingering—on the people of Iraq. The student also
is active in the movement to support the Palestinian struggle for
self-determination, and the day she came to see me was during a

period in which Israeli attacks on Palestinians were intensifying. We talked for some time about a number of political topics, but the conversation kept coming back to one main point: She hurt. As she was learning more about the suffering of others around the world, she felt that pain. What does one do about such a feeling, knowing that one's own government is either responsible for, or complicit in, so much of it? How does one stop feeling that pain, she asked.

I asked her whether she really wanted to wipe that feeling out of her life. Surely you know people, perhaps fellow students, who don't seem to feel that pain, who ignore all that suffering, I told her. Do you want to become like them? No matter how much it hurts, would you rather not feel at all? Would you rather be willfully ignorant about what is happening? I could see tears welling in her eyes and feel them in my own; it was an emotional moment for both of us. She left my office, not feeling better in any simplistic sense. But I hope she left at least with a sense that she was not alone and did not have to feel like a freak for feeling so much, so deeply.

A couple of hours later another student came by. After dealing with the classroom issue she wanted to discuss, we talked more generally about her interests in scientific research and the politics of funding research. I made the obvious point that profit-potential had a lot to do with what kind of research gets done. Certainly the comparative levels of research-and-development money that went, for example, to Viagra compared with money for drugs to combat new strains of TB tells us something about the values of our society, I suggested. The student agreed, but raised another issue. Given the overpopulation problem, she said, would it really be a good thing to spend lots of resources on developing those drugs? About halfway through her sentence I knew where she was heading, though I didn't want to believe it. This very bright student wanted to discuss whether it made sense to put resources into life-saving drugs for poor people in the Third World, given that there are arguably too many people on the planet already, or at least too many poor people in the Third World.

I contained my anger, somewhat, and told the student that when she was ready to sacrifice members of her own family to help solve the global population problem, then I would listen to her argument. In fact, given the outrageous levels of consumption of the middle and upper classes in the United States, I said, one could argue that large-scale death in the American suburbs would be far more beneficial in solving the population problem; a single U.S. family is more of a burden ecologically on the planet than a hundred Indian peasants. "If you would be willing to let an epidemic sweep through your hometown and kill large numbers of people without trying to stop it, for the good of the planet, then I'll listen to that argument," I said.

The student left shortly after that. Based on her reaction, I suspect I made her feel bad. I am glad for that. I wanted her to see that the assumption behind her comment—that the lives of people who look like her are more valuable than the lives of the poor and vulnerable in other parts of the world—was ethnocentric, racist, and barbaric. That assumption is the product of an arrogant and inhumane society. I wanted her to think about why she lived in a world in which the pain of others is so routinely ignored. I wanted her to feel what, for most of her life, she has been able to turn away from. I wanted her to begin to empathize with people who aren't white like her and not comfortable like her, people whose suffering is far away from her.

I do not want to overestimate the power of empathy to

change the world. But without empathy, without the ability to move outside our own experience, there is no hope of changing the world. Andrea Dworkin, one of the most important feminist thinkers of our time, has written, "The victims of any systematized brutality are discounted because others cannot bear to see, identify, or articulate the pain."[76] It is long past the time for all of us to start to see, to identify, to articulate the pain of systematized brutality. It is time to recognize that much of that pain is the result of a system designed to ensure our pleasures.

The pain of cluster bombs

It is my experience that people can feel empathy for the pain of others in certain situations, such as the pain of a loved one or friend, or in certain cases the suffering of people far away who are hit by a natural disaster or cruel twist of fate. But the key in Dworkin's insight is "systematized brutality." Empathy seems less forthcoming for those victims, especially when it is one's own government or society or culture that is systematizing the brutality. When the pain is caused by our government, we are channeled away from that empathy. The way we are educated and entertained keeps us from knowing about or understanding the pain of others in other parts of the world, and from understanding how our pleasure is connected to the pain of others. It is a combined intellectual, emotional, and moral failure—a failure to know, to feel, and to act.

Let's take a simple example, the CBU-87, also known as the cluster bomb, which is a part of the U.S. arsenal (along with other cluster munitions that are delivered by surface rocket or artillery).

---

[76] Andrea Dworkin, *Heartbreak: The Political Memoir of a Feminist Militant* (New York: Basic Books, 2002), p. 193.

It is a bomb that U.S. pilots drop from U.S. planes paid for by U.S. tax dollars. Each cluster bomb contains 202 individual submunitions, called bomblets (BLU-97/B). The CBU-87s are formally known as Combined Effects Munitions (CEM) because each bomblet has an antitank and antipersonnel effect, as well as an incendiary capability. The bomblets from each CBU-87 are typically distributed over an area roughly 100 by 50 meters, though the exact landing area of the bomblets is difficult to control.

As the soda can–size bomblets fall, a spring pushes out a nylon "parachute" (called the decelerator), which stabilizes and arms the bomblet. The BLU-97 is packed in a steel case with an incendiary zirconium ring. The case is made of scored steel designed to break into approximately 300 preformed thirty-grain fragments upon detonation of the internal explosive. The fragments then travel at extremely high speeds in all directions. This is the primary antipersonnel effect of the weapon. Antipersonnel means that the steel shards will shred anyone in the vicinity.

The primary antiarmor effect comes from a molten copper slug. If the bomblet has been properly oriented, the downward-firing charge travels at 2,570 feet per second and is able to penetrate most armored vehicles. The zirconium ring spreads small incendiary fragments. The charge has the ability to penetrate 5 inches of armor on contact. The tiny steel case fragments are also powerful enough to damage light armor and trucks at 50 feet, and to cause human injury at 500 feet. The incendiary ring can start fires in any combustible environment.

Human Rights Watch, the source for this description,[77] is one of many groups that has called for a global moratorium on

---

[77] http://www.hrw.org/backgrounder/arms/cluster-bck1031.htm

use of cluster bombs because they cause unacceptable civilian casualties. Those casualties come partly in combat, because the munitions have a wide dispersal pattern and cannot be targeted precisely, making them especially dangerous when used near civilian areas. Even more deadly is the way in which cluster bombs don't work. The official initial failure-to-explode rate for the bomblets is 5 to 7 percent, though some de-mining workers estimate that up to 20 percent do not explode. That means in each cluster bomb from ten to forty of the bomblets fail to explode on contact as intended, becoming land mines that can be set off by a simple touch. Human Rights Watch estimates that more than 1,600 Kuwaiti and Iraqi civilians have been killed, and another 2,500 injured, by the estimated 1.2 million cluster bomb duds left following the 1991 Persian Gulf War. For decades after the Vietnam War, reports came in of children and farmers setting off bomblets. The weapons were also used in the NATO attack on Serbia and the U.S. attack on Afghanistan.

Both British and U.S. forces in the Iraq War used cluster munitions, including versions fired from artillery. British military officials say their cluster munitions use a different fuse system that cuts the dud rate to 2 percent. U.S. officials said that retrofitting the U.S. arsenal in this fashion would be too expensive. The army officer in charge of the program acknowledged there have been major improvements, but "it's just that they're not fielded yet." As a result, the cluster dud rate in the 2003 Iraq War was about the same as in the 1991 Gulf War.[78] After the war, a newspaper reported that U.S. military officials were rethinking

---

[78] Thomas Frank, "Officials: Hundreds of Iraqis killed by faulty grenades," *Newsday*, June 22, 2003.

the widespread use of cluster munitions—not on humanitarian grounds but because the duds "significantly impeded American troops' battlefield maneuverability," rendering "significant swaths of battlefield off limits to advancing U.S. troops."[79]

What does all this mean in real terms? It means that Abdul Naim's father is dead. The family's fields in the village of Rabat, a half hour from Herat in western Afghanistan, were sown with cluster bombs, some of the 1,150 reportedly used in Afghanistan. Some of the farmers tried to clear their fields; some of them died trying. Out of desperation, Naim said his father finally decided to take the chance. Using a shovel, the farmer cast three bomblets aside successfully. The fourth exploded. The shrapnel caught him in the throat.[80]

Or consider this testimony from a thirteen-year-old boy in Kosovo: "I went with my cousins to see the place where NATO bombed. As we walked I saw something yellow—someone told us it was a cluster bomb. One of us took it and put it into a well. Nothing happened . . . We began talking about taking the bomb to play with and then I just put it somewhere and it exploded. The boy near me died and I was thrown a meter into the air. The boy who died was fourteen—he had his head cut off." The thirteen-year-old lived, but with both his legs amputated.[81]

When one brings up these unpleasant facts, a common response is that "war is hell," that in war "people die and things

---

[79] Michael M. Phillips and Greg Jaffe, "Pentagon rethinks use of cluster bombs," *Wall Street Journal*, August 25, 2003, p. A4.

[80] Suzanne Goldenberg, "Long after the air raids, bomblets bring more death," *Guardian* (UK), January 28, 2002, p. 12.

[81] Richard Norton-Taylor, "Cluster Bombs: The Hidden Toll," Manchester *Guardian* (UK), August 2, 2000.

get broken." In response to questions about cluster bombs during the 2003 war, the chairman of the Joint Chiefs of Staff acknowledged that "it's unfortunate that we had to make those choices about hitting targets in civilian areas, but as we've said before as well, war is not a tidy affair, it's a very ugly affair."[82]

In this case, the "ugly affair" means that fourteen-year-olds die and thirteen-year-olds get broken. We are supposed to brush that aside. We are not supposed to feel. Such is war. Such is life during wartime. While it is true that, as Gulf War–era Pentagon spokesman Pete Williams put it, "There's no nice way to kill somebody in a war," it is also true that there are ways to fight a war without cluster bombs. There are ways to fight wars in which fewer fourteen-year-olds get killed.

One of the central concepts in international law, in the law of warfare, is that civilians shall not be targeted. That means not only a prohibition against intentionally killing civilians, but as the Geneva Conventions state, against attacks that are indiscriminate. Article 51's description of indiscriminate attacks is: "those which employ a method or means of combat the effects of which cannot be limited as required by this Protocol; and consequently, in each such case, are of a nature to strike military objectives and civilians or civilian objects without distinction." That's a cluster bomb.

Cluster bombs are made by Alliant Techsystems of Minnesota. I'm from that part of the country. There's a term

---

[82] "DoD News Briefing—Secretary Donald Rumsfeld and General Richard Myers," U.S. Department of Defense News Transcript, April 25, 2003. http://www.dod.gov/transcripts/2003/tr20030425-secdef0126.html

widely used there about the friendliness of Minnesotans, who are legendary for avoiding conflict (at least open conflict)— "Minnesota nice." Alliant employs 11,200 people, most of whom are no doubt nice. Many of the military personnel who drop cluster bombs and defend the use of cluster bombs are no doubt nice. Many of the U.S. citizens who don't seem to mind that we drop cluster bombs are no doubt nice. Minnesota nice. United States nice.

I wonder what the thirteen-year-old boy in Kosovo with no legs thinks about how nice we are?

I talk about cluster bombs as often as I can in front of as many audiences as possible. I want people to think about the thirteen-year-old boy with no legs and his cousin whose head was ripped off. I want as many people as possible in the United States to carry images like this in their head. I want people to know that the U.S. government's quest for global power, and the U.S. military's barbaric efforts to achieve that, leave thirteen-year-olds with no legs and memories of dead cousins. When officials and generals say we are fighting for freedom, I want people to think of cluster bombs. I want people to ask, "Whose freedom we are fighting for?" I want people to remember that our tax dollars paid for those cluster bombs.

If the capacity for empathy is part of what makes us human, what are we to do with that image, that boy's pain, the pain of the family members? If we had to face them, what would we say? If we had to face them, would we cry with them? Should we have to travel to Kosovo to feel that? Should we feel that simply based on what we know?

We know. We feel. Then we confront the question, how shall we act? Will we act?

The costs of our pleasures

Most people in the United States take for granted a standard of living that the vast majority of the world can barely imagine and can never expect to enjoy. Many of us can recite the figure that the United States is about 5 percent of the world's population yet we consume about 25 percent of the world's oil and 30 percent of the gross world product. How is that related to foreign policy and military intervention?

The clearest statement of the connection came in February 1948 in a classified U.S. State Department document, known as Policy Planning Staff memorandum 23. The policy paper had been drafted by George Kennan, the first director of the State Department's Policy Planning Staff. In the section on Asia, Kennan wrote:

> Furthermore, we have 50% of the world's wealth but only 6.3% of the population. This disparity is particularly great between ourselves and the peoples of Asia. In this situation, we cannot fail to be the object of envy and resentment. Our real task in the coming period is to devise a pattern of relationships which will permit us to maintain this position of disparity without positive detriment to our national security. To do so we will have to dispense with all sentimentality and daydreaming; and our attention will have to be concentrated everywhere on our immediate national objectives. We need not deceive ourselves that we can afford the luxury of altruism and world-benefaction.

Kennan argued for restraint in U.S. policy in the Far East, acknowledging the limits on the U.S. ability to dictate policy to nations in the region, particularly China and India. He went on to say:

We should stop putting ourselves in the position of being our brothers' keeper and refrain from offering moral and ideological advice. We should cease to talk about vague and—for the Far East—unreal objectives, such as human rights, the raising of living standards, and democratization. The day is not far off when we are going to have to deal in straight power concepts. The less we are then hampered by idealistic slogans, the better.[83]

Kennan advocated ditching the idealistic slogans about freedom, but it turned out those slogans were too effective for U.S. policymakers to give up. Still, Kennan's statement embodies the philosophy of a small elite sector of the United States whose goal is subordinating the interests of other peoples to the profit needs of American corporations. Most of us are not part of that sector. But although this nation's foreign policy and wars are designed to benefit an extremely small sector of the country, the general affluence of the culture is an important part of how those elites win support for those policies and wars. That is, people in working- and middle-class America who live comfortably have come to believe that their continued comfort depends on U.S. dominance around the world. Is that why so many working- and middle-class Americans are generally willing to support policies and wars of dominance, to protect that comfort? If leaders can propose a relatively cost-free way (that is, few American casualties and limited expenditures) to continue that dominance and ensure continued material comfort, will

---

[83] "Review of Current Trends/U.S. Foreign Policy," Report by the Policy Planning Staff, February 24, 1948, *Foreign Relations of the United States 1948*, Vol. 1, Part 2, pp. 524–525.

most Americans continue to endorse it, especially when the deeply ingrained mythology about how the United States fights for freedom can be tapped?

If that is true, then in addition to being able to face the pain of the world, we also need to reduce our own pleasures. The degree to which people believe they must keep consuming at this level to be happy will tend to distort the ability to see the degree to which our pleasures require others' pain. I believe the level of consumption in this country can only be maintained if people in other places (and increasingly a growing number of people here at home) suffer deprivation. By any standard, the level of poverty in the world is a moral outrage; more than a fifth of the world's people still live in abject poverty (under $1 a day), and about half live below the barely more generous standard of $2 a day;[84] at least half the world cannot meet basic expenditures for food, clothing, shelter, health, and education. More than 840 million people were undernourished in 1999–2001, with world hunger on the rise in the last half of the 1990s.[85] The sources of poverty, like the causes of most social/political phenomena, are complex. But at the heart of worldwide inequality today is the continued economic domination of the underdeveloped world by the developed world — with U.S. trade, foreign, and military policy square at the center of that system of domination. We are helping keep the poor of the world poor.

---

[84] U.N. Report on the High-Level Panel for the Financing of Development, 2001, http://www.un.org/reports/financing/summary.htm

[85] Food and Agriculture Organization, "The State of Food Insecurity in the World 2003," http://www.fao.org/docrep/006/j0083e/j0083e00.htm

I cannot say with great precision what a sustainable level of consumption is, nor can anyone else. I have taken steps to reduce my consumption, but it may turn out that I will have to take far more drastic steps. In fact, it almost certainly will turn out that way. But what is readily evident is that the standard middle-class lifestyle in the United States is unsustainable over the long term and, if that lifestyle were lived by all people in the world, it would be the end of life on the planet. If everyone in the world lived as we of privilege in the United States live, the game would be over. As U.N. Environment Program head Klaus Toepfer pointed out, China's aim of quadrupling its economy by 2020 can occur only if developed nations radically change their consumption habits to free up scarce resources for the world's poor. For example, if China had the same density of private cars as Germany, it would have to produce 650 million vehicles—a target that the world's supply of metal and oil could not sustain.[86]

There also are self-interested reasons for reducing our consumption. In many ways this high-energy, high-consumption lifestyle actually keeps people from being able to experience joy. How much happiness is there in a shopping mall? Reducing one's dependence on material comforts not only is a good in itself for oneself, but also can be part of a political project of creating a world in which most people will have less motivation to support unjust foreign policy and wars of domination. We need to begin the long process of taking apart a way of living that is grotesquely wasteful and based on unjustifiable disparities, not only because it is right in itself and in our own self-interest to do

---

[86] "China growth aims environmentally impossible," Reuters News Service, July 16, 2003.

so but because that affluence tends to divert people from seeing how their affluence is made possible by brutal policies abroad (and increasingly at home).

At this point, many people will argue that such attention to questions of personal choices is diversionary, or that adequate resources exist for all 6 billion people on the planet to live healthy lives, or that technology will solve the problems that our high-energy, high-consumption lifestyle creates. Such arguments, I believe, are nothing more than obfuscation based in fear. These personal choices will end up being insignificant without engaging in a larger political struggle to change the structure of society, but they are complementary; one can't go forward without the other.

Political action

We need to push these questions of pain and pleasure because knowing and feeling can lead to acting, to collective political action. The goal is not simply to feel, to sink into despair, to allow the pain to paralyze us, or to feel guilty about our affluence and become paralyzed by that guilt. The goal is to transform our society and take the U.S. boot off the neck of people around the world trying to transform their own societies. If we think of the boy with no legs and cry, that's okay. But we should remember the words of the great Cuban writer and revolutionary Jose Marti. Before he was killed by the Spanish for the crime of resisting Spanish rule, he said, "When others are weeping blood, what right have I to weep tears?"

Maybe we don't have a right to weep in the United States. Given how comfortably the vast majority of us live, maybe we long ago forfeited that right. But whether or not I have a right to weep, I do. There is nothing noble about my tears; in some sense, they are self-indulgent. They are my way of reminding myself that I am a person, that I haven't completely given up my humanity.

But our tears can be more than self-indulgent, if they motivate us to act. We cannot stop all the pain of the world. We all know that simply being alive means we will feel the pain of disappointment, disease, death. We all will watch loved ones grow old and die. We will be let down by friends we trust, and have to face the fact that we have done the same. That is part of the human condition. But cluster bombs are not inherently part of the human condition. Wars for domination and wars to protect privilege are not inherently part of the human condition. The fact that such wars have been with us for so long does not mean they must be with us forever.

These things can be changed by people committed to changing them. We can organize to force the government to stop using cluster bombs. We can organize to force the government to stop fighting the wars for domination in which cluster bombs are used. Eventually we can organize to change the institutions that drive the wars for domination. There is a better world to be built. It is a world we can get to only if we confront the pain produced by this domination. It is a world in which we will have to learn to experience pleasure in very different ways.

Cluster bombs are not an inherent part of the human condition. But empathy is. The capacity for change is, in all of us. But these things are not automatic. The question is: Will we choose to know, to feel, and to act? The question is: Are we strong enough to sustain hope?

HOPE

A FTER AN ANTIWAR talk in which I sharply criticized U.S. foreign policy, a student asked me, "Don't you find it hard to
live being so cynical?" When I responded that I thought my
comments were critical but not cynical, he asked, "But how can
being so critical not make you cynical?"

The student was equating any critique of injustice produced by
institutions and systems of power with cynicism about people.
His question made me realize how easy is cynicism and how
difficult is sustained critique in this culture, which shouldn't
surprise us. People with power are perfectly happy for the population to be cynical, because that tends to paralyze people and
leads to passivity. Those same powerful people also do their best
to derail critique—the process of working to understand the
nature of things around us and offering judgments about them—
because that tends to energize people and leads to resistance.
Understanding the difference between critique and cynicism—
and the difference between hope and optimism—is crucial to the
future of any struggle against injustice.

At this moment in history, those struggles must not only be
about trying to win changes in policies but also about the rein-

vigoration of public life—a call for participation, for politics, for radical citizenship in reactionary times. Radical and reactionary in this sense are not used to describe specific political positions, left versus right, but instead describe an approach not just to politics, narrowly defined, but to the central questions of what it means to be a human being in connection with others. The world we live in is reactionary because it is trying to squeeze those important human dimensions out of us in the political sphere and constrict the range of discussion so much that politics does seem to many to be useless. To resist that one must be radical, be political, and be radical in public politically.

To explain this I will describe my own journey from cynicism to hope, my own struggle both for greater understanding of myself and an understanding of something greater than me. This requires talking of love and justice, which means taking a small risk that I will be seen as naive or self-indulgent or just plain silly. But here we should recall one of Che Guevara's most memorable thoughts: "At the risk of sounding ridiculous let me say that a revolutionary is guided by great feelings of love."

From cynicism to hope

Let me start the story when I was younger, in my teens and twenties. I saw that the world was in pretty awful shape. The United States had just ended its terrorist campaign in Southeast Asia—what we commonly call the Vietnam War—and was intensifying another by proxy in Central America; rich people seemed unconcerned that their luxury was built on the backs of the suffering of literally billions of poor people around the world; people were still getting kicked around simply because they were women or nonwhite or gay or different in some fashion; and many people seemed not to care that the ecosystem that sustained our lives was in collapse.

I looked around at all that, and I got cynical. Human beings, it seemed to me, were pretty unpleasant creatures. Human nature, I assumed, had to be pretty rotten for all this suffering to go on and on, generation after generation. Even with the advances in social justice—such as the end of slavery, greater recognition of the basic rights of women, and so on—it was hard to be upbeat moving out of the twentieth century, one of the most brutal and bloody in human history, into the twenty-first century, which promised to be just as, if not more, brutal. (With a taste of the expanded American empire in the twenty-first, it appears U.S. leaders will keep that promise.)

Being cynical appeared to have some advantages. I could step back from all the chaos and be hip. I could make jokes about how stupid people were. I could pretend not to care. I could turn away from the suffering of others because I, one of the hip and cynical, understood just how pathetic a species we were. I thought I was the one who saw it all so clearly.

I stayed cynical, and disengaged, for some time. The fact that I was working at newspapers didn't help; for journalists, cynicism is an occupational hazard that takes great intelligence and maturity to resist, and I didn't possess either quality in adequate amounts. So cynical I stayed, until I went to graduate school and was given the luxury of time to read, think, and study. Lots of people go to graduate school and become cynics, or their cynicism deepens; universities can do that to people. But I got lucky and met some exceptional people—many of them outside the university—who helped me see another way.

For me, that way began with feminism. I read a lot and listened to women. I started to learn not only about gender and sexism, but I also picked up a new way to understand the world, a new method of inquiry for examining the ideas and institutions that shape our world. I learned to look at how systems and structures of power operate. I learned to see past the surface to the core elements of those systems and structures. When I did that, I realized that things were far worse than I had thought— the world was in more trouble than I had ever imagined. I learned about new levels of suffering and oppression.

That's when I stopped being cynical and began to feel hopeful.

That may seem counterintuitive. How did a deepening sense of the scale and scope of injustice and suffering make me hopeful? The answer is simple. For all those years, I was cynical for two basic reasons: I had the wrong view of human nature, and I didn't understand how the world worked. I thought the evil and stupidity all around me were the product of an inherently evil and stupid human nature, and therefore I didn't see any way to fight against injustice. It all seemed beyond our control.

Once I started to understand the nature of illegitimate structures of authority, I realized that people (including me) were not inherently evil or stupid, and that human nature (including mine) was complex and sometimes maddening, but not inherently aimed at the destruction of the world. I came to realize that the authority structures that so bent our lives were powerful and deeply entrenched. I also realized that most of the channels that the dominant culture offered us for working to make the world a better place were themselves deeply embedded in those authority structures, so that often the solutions were part of the problem. I realized that the analysis and action that could save us had to be more radical than I ever could have imagined.

I also realized that at the moment in history in which I lived, there were relatively few people who would agree with any of this: People had begun to talk about a "postfeminist" age; the attacks on affirmative action and ethnic studies were emerging; the fall of the Berlin Wall "proved" that capitalism was the only possible economic system; and the United States was celebrating the slaughter of the Gulf War.

So, at the moment I realized the depth of the problem and the forces stacked against justice, I got hopeful. The hope comes not from some delusional state, but from what I would argue is a sensible assessment of the situation. Cynicism might be an appropriate reaction to injustice that can't be changed. Hope is an appropriate response to a task that, while difficult, is imaginable. And once I could understand the structural forces that produced injustice, I could imagine what a world without those forces — and hence without the injustice — might look like. And I could imagine what activities and actions and ideas it would take to get us there. And I could look around, and look back into history, and realize that lots of people have understood this and that I hadn't stumbled onto a new idea.

In other words, I finally figured out that I should get to work.

So hope emerged out of cynicism. I began to see the power of radical analysis and the importance of collective action. I began to take the long view, to see that we face a struggle, but that it is not a pointless struggle. The exact choices we should make as we struggle are not always clear, but the framework for making choices is there.

Hope and optimism

I have hope, but that does not mean I am optimistic.

Just as we have to distinguish between critique and cynicism, we have to realize that hope is not synonymous with optimism. I am hopeful, but I am not necessarily always optimistic, at least not about the short-term possibilities. These systems and structures of power, these illegitimate structures of authority, are deeply entrenched. They will not be dislodged easily or quickly. Optimism and pessimism should hang on questions of fact—we should be optimistic when the facts argue for optimism.

For example, I am against the illegitimate structure of authority called the corporation. I want to see different forms of economic organization emerge. I am hopeful about the possibilities but not optimistic that in my lifetime I will see the demise of capitalism, corporations, and wage slavery. Still, I will do certain things to work toward that.

The same can be said of the problem of U.S. aggression against innocent people in the rest of the world. Given the bloody record of the United States in the past sixty years and the seemingly limitless capacity of U.S. officials to kill without conscience, I must confess I am not optimistic that such aggression will stop anytime soon, in large part because those corporate structures that drive the killing are still around. But I will do certain things to work against it.

Or take the large state research university. I am concerned about how the needs of students are systematically ignored while the needs of corporate funders are privileged, how critical thinking is squashed not by accident but by design. I am concerned about the illegitimate structures of authority that I work in, which compel me to act in ways against the interests of students. I am not optimistic that the structure of big research universities is going to change anytime soon. But I will do certain things to work against the structures.

So, why would I do any of those things if my expectations of short-term success are so low? One reason is that I could be wrong about my assessment of the likelihood of change. I've been wrong about a lot of things in my life; the list grows every day. For all I know, corporate capitalism is on the verge of collapse, and if we just keep the pressure on it will start to unravel tomorrow. Or perhaps public discontent with murderous U.S. foreign policy is going to continue to expand and radicalize ever-larger numbers of people. Or perhaps the contradictions of these behemoth universities are becoming so apparent that the illegitimate structures of authority are about to give way to something that deserves the label "higher education."

History is too complex and contingent for any of us to make predictions. We simply don't have the intellectual tools to understand with much precision how and why people and societies change. History is a rough guide, but it offers no social-change equation. Still, there's really no reasonable alternative except to keep plugging away, constantly seeking to learn from mistakes and adapt to new conditions. Basically, there are two choices, which are common sense but that I didn't understand until I heard them articulated by Noam Chomsky: We can either predict the worst—that no change is possible—and not act, in which case we guarantee there will be no change. Or we can understand that change always is possible, even in the face of great odds, and act on that assumption, which creates the possibility of progress.[87]

Every great struggle for justice in human history began as a lost cause. When Gabriel Prosser made plans to take Richmond,

---

[87] See Chomsky's interview with Michael Albert at http://www.zmag.org/chomsky/interviews/9301-albchomsky-2.html

Virginia, in 1800, the first large-scale organized slave revolt, he was fighting a lost cause, for which he was hanged. When eight Quakers got together in 1815 to form the first white antislavery society in the United States (the Tennessee Society for the Manumission of Slaves) they were fighting a lost cause, but one that eventually carried the day. Where would we be today if Prosser and the Quakers had not acted?

The joy is in the struggle

But that can't be the only answer to the question "why should I be politically active?" We are human beings, not machines, and we all have needs. It is hard to sustain ourselves in difficult work if the only reward is the possibility that somewhere down the line our work may have some positive effect, though we may be long dead. That's a lot to ask of people. We all want more than that out of life. We want joy and love. At least every now and then, we want to have a good time, including a good time while engaged in our work. No political movement can sustain itself indefinitely without understanding that, not just because people need—and have a right—to be happy, but because if there is no joy in it, then movements are more likely to be dangerous. The joy—the celebration of being human and being alive in connection with others—is what fuels the drive for change.

People find joy in many different ways. As many people over the years have pointed out, one source of joy is in the struggle. I have spent a lot of time in the past few years doing political work, and some of that work isn't terribly fun. Collating photocopies for a meeting for a progressive political cause isn't any more fun than collating photocopies for a meeting for a corporate employer. But it is different in some ways: It puts you in contact with like-minded people. It sparks conversation. It creates space in which you can think and feel your way through difficult questions. It's a great place to laugh as you staple. It provides the context for connections that go beyond superficial acquaintanceships.

The joy is in the struggle, but not just because in struggle one connects to decent people. The joy is also in the pain of struggle. Joy is multilayered—one key aspect of it is discovery, and one way we discover things about ourselves and others is through pain. Pain can become part of joy when it is confronted. Struggle confronts pain. Struggle produces joy.

The joy is in the struggle. The struggle is not just the struggle against illegitimate structures of authority in the abstract. The struggles are in each of us—struggles to find the facts, to analyze clearly, to imagine solutions, to join with others in collective action for justice, and struggles to understand ourselves in relation to each other and ourselves as we engage in all these activities.

I realize that this struggle doesn't seem appealing to many. I have heard lots of people say that they can't cope with the complexity of politics. It seems too much, too big, too confusing. All they can handle, they say, is to focus on their individual lives and do the best to fix their lives. I have heard many parents say that their contribution to a better world is to raise their children with progressive values. That's all well and good; better to have children with progressive rather than reactionary role models. But I think these folks misunderstand not just their moral obligation but the nature of progress, individual and collective. We don't fix ourselves in isolation. We don't build decent lives by cutting ourselves off from problems just because they are complex. There are no private solutions to public problems. Yes, there are times when difficult situations force us to turn inward and deal with pressing problems in our lives. But I am arguing against the permanent division of our lives into these artificial categories. Our personal problems are never wholly individual, and hence they can't be fixed in individual ways. Part of the solution is always to be found in the bigger struggle, in which we all have a part.

I have learned that there is great joy in that bigger struggle, which leads us back to the abandonment of cynicism and the embrace of hope. Cynicism is a sophomoric and self-indulgent retreat from the world and all its problems. Hope is a mature and loving embrace of the world and all its promise. That does not mean one should have unfounded or naive hope. Wendell Berry reminds us that history shows that "massive human failure" is possible, but that "hope is one of our duties. A part of our obligation to our own being and to our descendants is to study our life and our condition, searching always for the authentic underpinnings of hope. And if we look, these underpinnings can still be found."[88]

Holding onto hope

Hope is one of our duties, but that does not mean it is always easy. There are many times, especially since 9/11, that it has been difficult to hold onto hope. The combination of seeing the World Trade Center towers fall, and then watching the unfolding of an illegal and immoral war on Afghanistan, and then watching the Bush administration move on to invade Iraq—all of that has tested my own sense of hope. At the same time that

---

[88] Wendell Berry, *Sex, Economy, Freedom & Community* (New York: Pantheon, 1993), p. 11.

I have been writing and thinking about the war, I also have been continuing my work on sexual violence and pornography.[89] Both spark the same feeling in my gut—despair over how cruel people, especially men, can be. When I have to face humans' willingness to inflict pain—and ability to find pleasure in inflicting pain—whether in the realm of the global or the intimate, some part of me wants to die; I can't bear it. Maybe some part of me does die.

But those authentic underpinnings of hope remain. On the day I was writing part of this, I had a meeting with a student on my campus who had read something I had written about the Afghanistan War and wanted to talk. She said she didn't have anything in particular to ask me. She just wanted to talk to someone who didn't think she was crazy. All around her at work and school, people   pro, con, or neutral—were refusing to talk about the war, she said. So we talked for a bit. We did politics, in a small way, the way politics is most often done. We talked about how she might organize a political group on campus. But maybe more important, we shored up each other's sense of hope. We could talk about the pain and craziness of the war without turning away.

Real hope—the belief in the authentic underpinnings of hope—is radical. A belief that people are not evil and stupid, not consigned merely to live out predetermined roles in illegitimate structures of authority, is radical. The willingness to act publicly on that hope and that belief is radical.

---

[89] "You are what you eat: The pervasive porn industry and what it says about you and your desires," *Clamor* magazine, September/October 2002, pp. 54–59.

We all live in a society that would prefer that we not be radical, that we not understand any of this. We live in a society that prefers productive but passive people. I work at a university that is part of that society, and has many of the same problems. Many classes at the university are either explicitly or implicitly designed to convince students that everything I have argued here is fundamentally crazy. The same goes for much of what comes to us through the commercial mass media. Some of what I say indeed may be misguided; as I said, I understand that I could be, and often am, wrong.

But, even if I'm wrong in some ways, I'd rather be wrong with hope than cynicism. I'd rather be naive than hip. I'd rather work for a just and sustainable world and fail than abandon the hope. I understand that this position is not wholly logical; it is based on a sense of how we can best make good on the gifts that come with being part of the human community. It is based on a faith in something common to us all, a capacity that is difficult to name, but which is perhaps best summed up by a phrase once used by the Brazilian educator Paulo Freire. Our task simply put, he said, is "to change some conditions that appear to me as obviously against the beauty of being human."[90]

In the end, that is the central hope: We can join together to help build not a utopia but a world in which we can struggle — individually and collectively, through the pain and with joy — to get as close as we can to the beauty of being human.

---

[90] Myles Horton and Paulo Freire, *We Make the Road by Walking* (Philadelphia: Temple University Press, 1990), p. 131.

CONCLUSION: A MOMENT FOUND?
Political Emotions: Despair and Alienation in the Empire

IN MANY WAYS, I am a typical white middle-class American. I have never lived outside the United States. I have traveled little outside North America. I speak only English. For personal and political reasons I expect to live out my life here. This country is, and feels like, my home. And yet I have never felt more alien in the United States. Since childhood I have always felt a bit out of step with the dominant culture of the United States, and that feeling has grown stronger as I have grown older. After 9/11—as my home has become a homeland—the alienation has peaked.

I have never been more distant from my peers. I have never felt so fundamentally alone so often. The community in which I feel comfortable has shrunk dramatically. When in "normal" settings, such as at work, I usually feel as if I live in some parallel universe. I have been less interested in attending routine social gatherings outside of my political cohort. I find myself more frequently communicating over e-mail with like-minded people in other cities rather than chatting with colleagues in the hallway. Instead of looking for ways to expand my social circle, I have let it contract.

There is no reason to pretend I don't feel this way, and from conversations with others around the country I know that many others feel similarly. The United States has taken an ugly turn since 9/11. Decent people should feel alienated; we have a right to feel that way. And at the same time—if we truly believe in creating an alternative to this ugly world—we cannot allow ourselves the luxury of alienation, nor can we wallow in our sense of being different. We must not separate ourselves from the larger world that creates this sense of being alone. If we do that—if those who want to resist the American empire cut ourselves off from the larger society—it will be the ultimate exercise of privilege.

That is the difficult position in which many of us who want to oppose the U.S. empire find ourselves: Our primary task is organizing people in the United States to resist imperial policies, the very people from whom we so often feel alienated and isolated. To think how to approach this, we first should be clear about our task.

Dismantling the empire

A serious movement must start with this reality: We citizens of the United States are citizens of the empire. One of the people most happy about that fact, *Atlantic Monthly* correspondent Robert Kaplan, has suggested we move beyond the obvious— "that the United States now possesses a global empire"—and start figuring out how to run it.[91] While many celebrate the empire, the reflections of one of Britain's most eminent historians, Eric Hobsbawm, are relevant here:

---

[91] Robert D. Kaplan, "Supremacy by stealth," *Atlantic Monthly*, July/August 2003, pp. 66–83.

The present world situation is unprecedented. The great global empires of the past—such as the Spanish and notably the British—bear little comparison with what we see today in the United States empire. A key novelty of the U.S. imperial project is that all other empires knew that they were not the only ones, and none aimed at global domination. None believed themselves invulnerable, even if they believed themselves to be central to the world—as China did, or the Roman empire. Regional domination was the maximum danger envisaged until the end of the cold war. A global reach, which became possible after 1492, should not be confused with global domination.

[T]the U.S., like revolutionary France and revolutionary Russia, is a great power based on a universalist revolution— and therefore on the belief that the rest of the world should follow its example, or even that it should help liberate the rest of the world. Few things are more dangerous than empires pursuing their own interest in the belief that they are doing humanity a favour.[92]

U.S. policymakers routinely take exception to that claim. Near the end of the Iraq War, Secretary of Defense Donald Rumsfeld stated flatly: "We don't seek empires. We're not imperialistic, we've never been."[93] But imperialism does not require the direct imposition of colonial relations. Again, quoting Hobsbawm: "Of course the Americans theoretically do not aim to occupy the whole world. What they aim to do is to go to war, leave friendly governments behind them and go home again."

[92] Eric Hobsbawm, "America's imperial delusion: The U.S. drive for world domination has no historical precedent," *The Guardian* (UK), June 14, 2003. http://www.guardian.co.uk/usa/story/0,12271,977470,00.html

[93] Jim Mannion, "Rumsfeld heaps praise on troops for Iraq victory," Agence France-Presse, April 28, 2003.

It matters little that we do not directly take ownership of territory and install colonial governors as did empires of the past; the modalities of control have changed, but not the goal of control. Although many still recoil at thinking of the United States as an imperial power, the facts are clear. The United States today has:

— global reach, in military, political, economic, and cultural terms;

— a social structure and value system oriented toward the accumulation of power and rationalization of vast disparities in consumption of resources;

— the technological means to subdue other societies to achieve those ends;

— at elite levels, a culture of barbarism in which leaders are willing to act outside of basic moral considerations; and

— a general population that, with the exception of a dissenting minority, either actively endorses or does nothing to stop the imperial project.

The empire works through military and economic power — through the use of the national military force to dictate the composition of governments (most recently in Afghanistan and Iraq) and binational or multinational organizations it dominates to dictate the terms of trade and investment (regional trade agreements, the World Trade Organization, International Monetary Fund, World Bank).

If one doubts the imperial intentions of the current government, consider this clear statement of the U.S. goal from the 2002 National Security Strategy document: "Our forces will be strong enough to dissuade potential adversaries from pursuing a military build-up in hopes of surpassing, or equaling, the power of the United States." To do that, "the United States will require bases and stations within and beyond Western Europe and Northeast Asia, as well as temporary access arrangements for the long-distance deployment of U.S. forces." Once deployed, the United States can accept no constraints on these forces: "We will take the actions necessary to ensure that our efforts to meet our global security commitments and protect Americans are not impaired by the potential for investigations, inquiry, or prosecution by the International Criminal Court (ICC), whose jurisdiction does not extend to Americans and which we do not accept."[94]

This plan requires what the military calls "full spectrum dominance," defined as "the ability of U.S. forces, operating unilaterally or in combination with multinational and inter-agency partners, to defeat any adversary and control any situation across the full range of military operations." In the military's terms, full spectrum dominance allows the United States to be "persuasive in peace," "decisive in war," and "preeminent in any form of conflict."[95] In other words, the goal is to be able to run the world, without significant challenge.

The consequences of this imperial project have been grim for many around the world — those who have been the targets of U.S. military power; those who have lived under repressive regimes backed by the United States; and those who toil in economies that are increasingly subordinated to the United States and multinational corporations. Scratch the surface of U.S. rhetoric about its

---

[94] The National Security Strategy of the United States of America.
http://www.whitehouse.gov/nsc/nssall.html

[95] Chairman of the Joint Chiefs of Staff, "Joint Vision 2020," June 2000.
http://www.dtic.mil/jointvision/jv2020.doc

quest to bring freedom and democracy to the world, and one finds the suffering of the people who must live with the reality of U.S. foreign policy. Like most empires, the United States claims to be pursuing noble goals abroad: peace, freedom, democracy. But U.S. actions show the real goal is to consolidate power and control resources. This is hardly surprising: Empires are inherently immoral, never designed to benefit the people in targeted countries (outside of an elite who cooperate with the imperial power to their own advantage). The material gains from the empire are concentrated at the top of the imperial country, with some benefits to a larger segment of society.

Therefore, there is always one central task for citizens in the empire: To be part of the process of taking apart the empire. History suggests that if we don't dismantle it from the inside, some force from the outside eventually will. On 9/11, we got a glimpse of what that might look like. So, there are two compelling arguments for citizens of the empire.

The first is an argument from justice. If we truly believe in democracy and justice, the use of force (economic or military) by one country against another would require a clear justification in the interests of the people of the targeted country. We would have to show that there is no other viable way for the lives of people in that country to be improved on crucial criteria—such as the right to a minimal standard of living or freedom from persecution—and that all possible solutions consistent with international law and basic morality have been exhausted. No such case has ever been made to justify U.S. imperialism. So, if we take seriously the demands of justice, we must resist the empire.

There is a second argument, from self-interest, which goes in two different directions. First, we have seen the predictable consequence of U.S imperial policies—the building of resentment against the United States. Given the overwhelming dominance of American military power, any force—for whatever reason—that wants to challenge the United States will have to use asymmetrical strategies; a direct military challenge is unthinkable. So, these countries, movements, and networks will use guerrilla strategies where the U.S. military is engaged, and/or terrorist strategies aimed at the U.S. population. When opponents cannot prevail by striking "hard" targets (the military), they will choose "soft" targets (civilians). So, if one truly wants to be more secure in living in the United States, one should join the antiwar and antiempire movement.

There is another important aspect to the argument from self-interest that is less tangible. As I argued in Chapter 6, U.S. dominance of the world helps maintain the affluence of our society, which provides most of us not only with a comfortable level of the basics to survive, but also lots of toys. Yet material comfort has not provided most people with the fulfillment that humans routinely seek, and more and more people are coming to terms with a simple but painful fact: A life built on consumption and comfort is not a complete life. There are always two paths that decent people must follow to move forward from that realization. One is to make changes in our personal lives, to disengage as much as possible from a consumerist culture that tries to force us to define ourselves through commodities. The other is to come together with others in political struggle to change the whole system. Both are important; neither is adequate by itself. If we take seriously this challenge, we can begin to see clearly the ways in which the system of capitalism and empire has colonized our own lives, our own ways of seeing the world. From that, there is hope we can dismantle the system that seeks to dictate terms to the whole world.

Dealing with triumphalism and apathy

This message of resistance to the empire is not an easy sell in the United States these days.

To one segment of the American public, these claims appear lunatic. Deeply invested in the political mythology discussed in Part I, many people are reveling in triumphalism: "Yes, the United States has emerged as an empire, and it's a good thing, too." From this view, the United States is the only force in the world capable of imposing order. Hence, imperialism is not only acceptable but morally required.

That imperial project is also widely considered to be the best way to make Americans more secure. Rather than examine the reasons the United States is targeted and address those reasons, many people endorse the response of brute force—as much as necessary. And in many circles, there is little interest in questioning the high-energy use, high-consumption lifestyle. As George W. Bush's press secretary put it when was asked in May 2001 whether Americans should "correct our lifestyles" to reduce energy consumption: "That's a big no. The President believes that it's an American way of life, and that it should be the goal of policymakers to protect the American way of life. The American way of life is a blessed one."[96]

Like many, I feel alienated from people who take these political and moral positions. But although it can be difficult to be around people who crow about how the United States "kicked

---

[96] Ari Fleischer, White House news briefing, May 7, 2001.

butt" in Iraq, in some ways those interactions are simple. When it is clear that a conversation is unlikely to be productive, I simply abandon the conversation. That's not defeatist, but rather an acknowledgment that in certain times and places there is no argument likely to be effective—in the short term—to a person rooted in such a radically different worldview. Sometimes, it makes sense to engage in a different kind of conversation with that person, and other times it is best to conserve one's energy for potentially more fruitful engagement.

The more difficult struggles for me—and the main cause of my increasing sense of isolation—come in dealing with people who seem detached, who don't react at all. There are a lot of people around me, especially in the university where I work, who seem to be doing their best to avoid questions of war and empire. In a small number of cases, this may stem from some fundamental amorality, from truly not caring. But my sense is that many of the people trying to avoid the question have some sort of antiwar leanings—they know there's something wrong with the way the United States has gone forward in the world since 9/11, especially in the Iraq War; if not against the wars, they are at least skeptical. But they seem determined to sleepwalk through life.

Those are the people I have the most trouble interacting with. When I raise the issue of war they sometimes attempt to divert the conversation toward less contentious subjects. More often people are willing to let me talk but refuse to engage, or sometimes refuse to even acknowledge what I am saying. There have been times I literally wanted to grab people and shout, "You know these wars are wrong! You know these policies are crazy! Why won't you help do something about it? Why won't you at least admit to me that you know?"

Like thousands of others around the country, for the past two years I have put more time and energy into political work than ever before in my life. And because I have been spending so much time organizing, writing, and speaking, I have taken it for granted that I was doing all that I could do. Because I have been working more than ever on a variety of political projects, it doesn't always occur to me to evaluate how my alienation affects the usefulness of that political activity. But that evaluation is crucial.

Sometimes this problem gets reduced to the charge that white middle-class activists simply are elitists who don't know how to interact with "real" people. That may be true in some cases, but it strikes me as a gross oversimplification and a way to avoid difficult questions. Yes, the antiwar movement has failed to broaden out significantly from its white, middle-class base. But the alienation I am talking about doesn't result primarily from class or race divisions; some of my most frustrating experiences have been with other white middle-class people. Instead, the dividing line is whether one is willing to confront the American ideology in public.

In such an environment, antiwar activists need to come together often, not just for political organizing but for support. We need to engage in internal discussions to sharpen our analysis and rethink strategy. But at the same time we need to be careful not to withdraw too much from these other spaces in our lives, even if they feel alien or alienating to us. Whether or not we are actively organizing in those spaces at the moment, it's important to stay rooted in the larger communities in which we live. The struggle against the U.S. empire will be a long one, and we need to be connected to the people we are trying to organize.

Public hope

The way out of that alienation is faith that a country protected by its power can relinquish some of that power; that a society insulated by its privilege from many of the consequences of the unjust use of power can renounce that privilege; that a people comfortable in their affluence can collectively work to change the system that makes them comfortable. It is a tall order. It requires not just a change in policies but in worldview. And, perhaps even more imposing, it eventually will require not just individual hope but the creation of public hope where now there is little.

I borrow the phrase from C. Douglas Lummis, who contrasts "public hope" with "private hope." Many of the people I describe above—Americans who might be skeptical and scared of U.S. imperial policies—have private hope; they believe that they will continue to enjoy a comfortable standard of living in a reasonably predictable world. But they also have no expectation that the political system can or will change to become more open or fair. By contrast, Lummis described the state of public hope and the atmosphere of freedom that was in the air everywhere in the Philippines in 1985, before the fall of the U.S.-backed Marcos dictatorship. There, a state of public despair was reversed:

> People begin to believe that public action can succeed. It doesn't matter why they believe it—it could be for the wrong reason. When hope is shared by many, it becomes its own reason. Public hope is itself grounds for hope. When many people, filled with hope, take part in public action, hope is transformed from near-groundless faith (which it was in the state of public despair) to plain common sense.[97]

[97] Lummis, *Radical Democracy* (Ithaca, NY: Cornell University Press, 1996), p. 156.

That is not a naive belief that if only enough people would be hopeful that things will change. The creation of public hope is a political project that requires analysis and organizing. That public hope begins with a group of people committed to change, clear about the goals, willing to take risks. To create such hope we must acknowledge our fears and come together collectively to overcome them. We must acknowledge our sense of alienation yet realize we have to overcome it if we are to build a movement powerful enough to make change. And we must balance having enough confidence in our analysis to propel us forward, while at the same time having the humility necessary to be open to errors we inevitably will make.

I have failed routinely at all these tasks—more often than anyone else knows, for I hide many of the failures out of shame. I have at various times let my fear overwhelm me. I have sunk too deeply into my own alienation. And I too often have succumbed to arrogance and hubris. But in the end, the measure of our contributions will not be how many times we fail, but how many times we find the strength to let others help us see our failures, find some way to learn from them, and move forward.

This requires faith, in ourselves and each other, and the courage to act on that faith.

Perhaps in the end, all politics is about where one chooses to put one's faith. Before 9/11, many Americans thought they could live in pampered isolation, draining the world's resources without having to be part of, or accountable to, the rest of the world. Many Americans felt beyond the reach of the pain of the rest of the world. After 9/11, such self-indulgence is no longer possible; we now know how vulnerable we all are. If in the past we were unmoved by moral arguments about how our comfort was built on so much suffering around the world, now there is a heightened measure of self-interest to be considered. It is difficult to ignore the fact that U.S. economic, military, and foreign policy must change. Our choices are fairly stark.

Where shall we put our faith? In the reactionary program of the Republican Party and George W. Bush's perverse "with us or with the terrorists" logic? Or in the kinder-and-gentler imperialism of the mainstream Democratic Party and its fake multilateralism? Or shall we put our faith in each other to find a way to stop living on top of the world and start living as part of the world?

Can we face the task of being citizens of the empire? Do we have the courage to stop being Americans and become human beings? Do we care enough about ourselves and the world to struggle to claim our humanity?

The rest of the world is waiting for our answer.

APPENDIX
Stop the Insanity Here
September 12, 2001[98]

September 11 was a day of sadness, anger, and fear.

Like everyone in the United States and around the world, I shared the deep sadness at the deaths of thousands.

But as I listened to people around me talk, I realized the anger and fear I felt were very different, for my primary anger is directed at the leaders of this country and my fear is not only for the safety of Americans but for innocents civilians in other countries.

It should need not be said, but I will say it: The acts of terrorism that killed civilians in New York and Washington were reprehensible and indefensible; to try to defend them would be to abandon one's humanity. No matter what the motivation of the attackers, the method is beyond discussion.

But this act was no more despicable than the massive acts of terrorism—the deliberate killing of civilians for political pur-

---

[98] The slightly modified version for the newspaper appeared as "U.S. guilty of committing own violent acts," *Houston Chronicle*, September 14, 2001, p. A-33. Text available at http://www.chron.com/cs/CDA/ story.hts/editorial/1047072

poses—that the U.S. government has committed during my lifetime. For more than five decades throughout the Third World, the United States has deliberately targeted civilians or engaged in violence so indiscriminate that there is no other way to understand it except as terrorism. And it has supported similar acts of terrorism by client states.

If that statement seems outrageous, ask the people of Vietnam. Or Cambodia and Laos. Or Indonesia and East Timor. Or Chile. Or Central America. Or Iraq, or Palestine. The list of countries and peoples who have felt the violence of this country is long. Vietnamese civilians bombed by the United States. Timorese civilians killed by a U.S. ally with U.S.-supplied weapons. Nicaraguan civilians killed by a U.S. proxy army of terrorists. Iraqi civilians killed by the deliberate bombing of an entire country's infrastructure.

So, my anger on this day is directed not only at individuals who engineered the September 11 tragedy but at those who have held power in the United States and have engineered attacks on civilians every bit as tragic. That anger is compounded by hypocritical U.S. officials' talk of their commitment to higher ideals, as President Bush proclaimed "our resolve for justice and peace."

To the president, I can only say: The stilled voices of the millions killed in Southeast Asia, in Central America, in the Middle East as a direct result of U.S. policy are the evidence of our resolve for justice and peace.

Though that anger stayed with me off and on all day, it quickly gave way to fear, but not the fear of "where will the terrorists strike next," which I heard voiced all around me. Instead, I almost immediately had to face the question: "When will the United States, without regard for civilian casualties, retaliate?" I wish the question were, "Will the United States retaliate?" But if history is a guide, it is a question only of when and where.

So, the question is which civilians will be unlucky enough to be in the way of the U.S. bombs and missiles that might be unleashed. The last time the U.S. responded to terrorism, the attack on its embassies in Kenya and Tanzania in 1998, it was innocents in the Sudan and Afghanistan who were in the way. We were told that time around they hit only military targets, though the target in the Sudan turned out to be a pharmaceutical factory.

As I monitored television during the day, the talk of retaliation was in the air; in the voices of some of the national-security "experts" there was a hunger for retaliation. Even the journalists couldn't resist; speculating on a military strike that might come, Peter Jennings of ABC News said that "the response is going to have to be massive" if it is to be effective.

Let us not forget that a "massive response" will kill people, and if the pattern of past U.S. actions holds, it will kill innocents. Innocent people, just like the ones in the towers in New York and the ones on the airplanes that were hijacked. To borrow from President Bush, "mothers and fathers, friends and neighbors" will surely die in a massive response.

If we are truly going to claim to be decent people, our tears must flow not only for those of our own country. People are people, and grief that is limited to those within a specific political boundary denies the humanity of others.

And if we are to be decent people, we all must demand of our government—the government that a great man of peace, Martin Luther King Jr., once described as "the greatest purveyor of violence in the world"—that the insanity stop here.

ADDITIONAL RESOURCES

A number of the ideas in this book were first published on web sites dedicated to progressive and radical politics. There are too many good sites to list them all, but these three have been particularly important to the movement.

ZNet
http://www.zmag.org/weluser.htm

Counterpunch
http://www.counterpunch.org/

Common Dreams News Center
http://www.commondreams.org/

The following political groups in the United States are carrying on important organizing work related to issues discussed in this book.

United for Peace and Justice
http://www.unitedforpeace.org/

Global Exchange
http://www.globalexchange.org/

U.S. Campaign to End the Israeli Occupation
http://www.endtheoccupation.org

National Network to End the War against Iraq/The Grassroots
Peace Network
http://www.endthewar.org

Institute for Public Accuracy
http://accuracy.org/

The following groups and programs offer valuable audio and video resources.

Media Education Foundation
http://www.mediaed.org/

Free Speech TV
http://www.freespeech.org/

Turning Tide Productions
http://www.turningtide.com/

Pacifica Radio
http://www.pacifica.org/

Democracy Now!
http://democracynow.org/

In addition to the information sources in footnotes, the following books offer important insights into U.S. politics and society, foreign policy, and mass media.

Berry, Wendell, *What Are People For?* (San Francisco: North
Point Press, 1990).

Blum, William, *Killing Hope: U.S. Military and CIA Interventions since World War II* (Monroe, ME: Common Courage Press, 1995).

Chomsky, Noam, *Understanding Power: The Indispensable Chomsky*, ed. Peter R. Mitchell and John Schoeffel (New York: New Press, 2002).

Churchill, Ward, *Perversions of Justice: Indigenous Peoples and Angloamerican Law* (San Francisco: City Lights Books, 2003).

Enloe, Cynthia, *Bananas, Beaches and Bases: Making Feminist Sense of International Politics* (Berkeley: University of California Press, 2001).

Herman, Edward S., *The Myth of the Liberal Media* (New York: Peter Lang, 2000).

Herman, Edward S., and Noam Chomsky, *Manufacturing Consent* (New York: Pantheon, 1988).

Jackson, Wes, *Becoming Native to this Place* (Washington, DC: Counterpoint Press, 1996).

Lorentzen, Lois Ann, and Jennifer Turpin, eds., *The Women and War Reader* (New York: New York University Press, 1998).

Loewen, James W., *Lies My Teacher Told Me* (New York: Simon and Schuster, 1995).

Mahajan, Rahul, *Full Spectrum Dominance: U.S. Power in Iraq and Beyond* (New York: Seven Stories, 2003).

Mahajan, Rahul, *The New Crusade: America's War on Terrorism* (New York: Monthly Review Press, 2002).

McChesney, Robert W., and John Nichols, *Our Media Not Theirs: The Democratic Struggle against Corporate Media* (New York: Seven Stories, 2002).

Pilger, John, *The New Rulers of the World* (London: Verso, 2002).

Rampton, Sheldon, and John Stauber, *Weapons of Mass Deception: The Uses of Propaganda in Bush's War on Iraq* (New York: Jeremy P. Tarcher/Penguin, 2003).

Zinn, Howard, *A People's History of the United States*, rev. ed. (New York: HarperPerennial, 1995).

ABOUT THE AUTHOR

R OBERT JENSEN IS an associate professor of journalism at the
University of Texas at Austin, where he has taught courses
on media law, ethics, and politics since 1992. He is the author of
*Writing Dissent: Taking Radical Ideas from the Margins to the
Mainstream* (Peter Lang, 2001), co-author with Gail Dines and
Ann Russo of *Pornography: The Production and Consumption of
Inequality* (Routledge, 1998); and co-editor with David S. Allen
of *Freeing the First Amendment: Critical Perspectives on Freedom
of Expression* (New York University Press, 1995). Jensen is a
founding member of the Nowar Collective (http://www.nowar-
collective.com) and a member of the board of the Third Coast
Activist Resource Center (http://thirdcoastactivist.org). He also
writes for popular media, and his opinion and analytic pieces on
foreign policy, politics, and race have appeared in *USA Today,
Los Angeles Times, Philadelphia Inquirer, Newsday, Houston
Chronicle, Dallas Morning News, Atlanta Journal-Constitution,
The Hindu* (India), *Al-Ahram* (Cairo), *The Progressive,* and on
web sites including Alternet, Common Dreams, Counterpunch,
and ZNet.